BERKONOMICS

Lessons from a Lifetime in 140 Characters or Less

Dave Berkus

Published by David Berkus.

For corrections, company/title updates, comments, or any other inquiries, please e-mail DBerkus@berkus.com

First Printing, 2009
10 9 8 7 6 5 4 3 2

ISBN number 978-0-557-14327-6

Material in this book is for educational purposes only. This book is sold with the understanding that neither the author nor the publisher are engaged in rendering legal, accounting, investment, or any other professional service. Neither the publisher nor the author assumes any liability for any errors or omissions, or for how this book or its contents are used or interpreted, or for any consequences resulting directly or indirectly from the use of this book. For legal advice or any other, please consult your personal lawyer or the appropriate professional.

Material in this book was serialized, previously published in the blog, *Berkonomics.com*, by the author.

Groups may order copies of the book at a group discount by contacting Dave Berkus at 626-355-5375, or at <u>dberkus@berkus.com</u> .

A companion workbook, *"The BERKONOMICS WORKBOOK"*, is available from the same sources where this book was purchased for use within Berkus workshops, and by readers to connect these insights with their own experiences and to form a guide for personal and corporate action.

Throughout this book, the Cambria type font was used for headlines, and text was set using the Calibri font.

The views expressed by the individuals in this book do not necessarily reflect the views shared by the companies they are employed by (or the companies mentioned in) this book. The employment status and <u>affiliations</u> of author with the companies referenced are subject to change.

Contents

INTRODUCTION

This book is more than a labor of love. It is the result of insights gained in over fifty years as an entrepreneur, fifteen of them investing in other entrepreneurs with world-changing ideas and passion enough to move mountains. Over seventy times I've bet on one or a group of those entrepreneurs, each time finding new stories and new insights to add to my caldron of entrepreneurial goop.

When I speak as a keynoter at entrepreneurial or investor conferences, or when I conduct one of my half day seminars in early stage corporate governance, I weave some of these epoch stories of entrepreneurs good and bad into my presentations (of course leaving the names out the stories). And universally, my audiences come back to me with comments that they remember and internalize the stories - and these short insights.

Along came the social networks and the tolerance for a story-in-a-second, or if not in a second, then in 140 characters or less. The entrepreneurial success stories didn't get shorter, but the insights became sharper. Is this the new communication norm? Should all professors of business now find ways to communicate in the verbal shorthand of the Twitter generation? Can a teacher push out enough information and expressed passion for a subject in such a short burst?

I thought it was worth a try. And so *Berkonomics* was born, partly of necessity to adapt to the shortened attention span of a young generation of entrepreneurs, and partly in an attempt to create memorable, repeatable, viral transfers of insight to this new audience of easily distracted but completely dedicated business professionals.

Like a small stream feeds the rivers into an ocean, these short bursts have been parsed into arbitrary, random groups of 101 insights further divided into eleven stages of a business from ignition to liquidity (startup to sale). The sum of these, the ocean of insight, is *Berkonomics*. The name was created by several members of the receiving audience, a number of whom began to call these *"Berkusisms"*, a much harder name to pronounce, let alone remember.

Yes, I wanted to call this collection "Nuggets", as in "nuggets of insight." It didn't take but seconds for a number of these young student-coaches to point out that the word has many connotations, some of which are unflattering to the idea of business insights, some of which are downright objectionable.

So we have a name and we have a style. How do we feed the streams into the rivers that roll into the ocean of content? We start with a tweet, a Facebook posting, a Plaxo or LinkedIn post. Each leads to a link to www.Berkonomics.com, where a bit more space is devoted to each burst for those with the time and inclination to explore more. The ocean in this case is this book, *Berkonomics*, containing the same 101 compact ideas further expanded with stories about entrepreneurs and their businesses that have embraced or violated these rules, these insights, and created an opportunity to tell yet another story to reinforce one of the lessons in business insight represented by the whole of this effort.

As you'll note from the very first of these brief essays in a sentence, flexibility and coachability are requirements for every good entrepreneur as well as those who choose to take this journey into the depths of business creation through these tweets, postings, blogs and book.

Every one of us has a story to add to this mix, one of passionate entrepreneurism, sometimes inside an existing larger corporation, sometimes alone on a kitchen table or back room desk. And it is a sure thing that many of us will have cogent, insightful additions to this caldron, culled from their own experiences. There's a place for these in the blog, www.berkonomics.com, and I welcome any and all for others to read and learn.

This adventure we call *Berkonomics* should be fun and informative. Let's all try to add a bit of each and stir the brew in the process.

Chapter One. IGNITION

1. Be flexible. Be coachable.

As an early stage investor, the first test for me is whether the entrepreneur is flexible in both the plan and execution of his or her vision (since from experience almost everything about a business plan changes over time), and whether the entrepreneur, no matter what age or experience, is coachable.

Doctoral theses have been written on this subject. Early stage investor groups often list these traits at or near the top of their list when filtering opportunities for investment. And I have numerous stories from personal experience that reinforce these two traits as the most positive indicators of future success in business.

In my book, *"Extending the Runway"* (Aspatore Press, 2006), I explore the thesis that there are five basic types of resources an entrepreneur must exploit in growing a successful business: **time, money, process, relationships and context**. Understanding the effects of each upon an entrepreneur and early stage business plan is critical. Being able to adapt to the realities and changes in the fast-moving environment is essential.

Flexibility: the context in which a business plan envisions the enterprise in its marketplace is constantly changing as new products and services challenge competitors to innovate and adapt. A plan written last month may easily need tweaking this month to recognize changes in the marketplace, the central context of the plan itself. Everything happens faster these days than even a few years ago, especially in the arena of technology, where many new businesses are developed each month to solve problems or take advantage of opportunities that existed at the moment of an entrepreneur's vision for the future.

And the money and time required to bring the young company from idea to market extends out as changes require rethinking the plan. We'll explore this reality in later insights as we explore the stages of business development.

One of the best indicators of future success for an entrepreneur and an early stage idea is the quality and depth of great relationships with industry veterans or technology gurus, or experienced successful business leaders. Those relationships would be impressive but worthless if the entrepreneur was not coachable, open to suggestion and criticism from those who have experience enough to surface the issues unspoken but obvious to the coach.

And finally, there are always ways to improve the process of design, test, roll-out and marketing a new idea. And many potential coaches out there have made mistakes in these processes at the expense of their employers or even their personal savings. Since we all learn from our mistakes, it seems reasonable that we should learn from the mistakes of others, particularly those who freely offer their experiences as lessons for our enterprise.

I've seen entrepreneurs go through the complete process of raising money for a business from investors, many of whom were experienced and well beyond just friends and family, only to ignore all advice and execute a flawed business plan to death, ignoring the pleas and attempts at coaching by others including those investors.

Don't be one of those. Be flexible and be coachable.

2. Management quality trumps a quality plan.

Great management teams mean more to investors than even greater business plans.

If flexibility and coachability are first in the list of traits investors value in an entrepreneur, then the quality of the proposed or actual management team come in a close second, even before the attractiveness of the business plan itself. The quest for a great management team is not a fluke, but rather a result of backward looks at the failure rate from past investments by angel investors and venture capitalists.

It is true that at least half of the businesses backed by professional early stage investors will die within three years or less. That reality is a tough one for the professional investor, almost as tough as for those entrepreneurs who lose their businesses. The latter can start new businesses, flush with the experiences gained from the previous effort and much the better for it. The investor's cash is lost forever, and the experience gained usually is just another increment in a list of similar experiences from the past.

It is the management team, most often led by a passionate entrepreneur with experience in the industry, which makes the biggest difference between success and failure, even for businesses built upon less than sterling basic ideas. Among professional investors, almost all would rather back a great team with an average idea before a great idea and inexperienced team. It comes back to coachability and flexibility, our first insight. Great teams are flexible and have the advantage of experience in seeing the pitfalls before them from their past. They are coachable in that they have taken advantage of the vast experience of others in overcoming obstacles and finding ways to speed a product to market faster or create a service whose quality exceeds that of the competition.

None of this is to say that an inexperienced entrepreneur cannot lead a great new business. But it would be foolish to try without surrounding himself with as many experienced co-leaders as possible from the outset. As a start, such an entrepreneur will soon "know what he (she) doesn't know", an important qualifier for success in any business endeavor, when combined with the willingness to fill gaps in knowledge with help from those who have the experience to do so.

Ask any professional investor, and you should hear that they value the quality of the team above the attractiveness of the early drafts of the business plan. Even without taking in money from professional investors, that advice would serve you well in protecting your own monetary investment.

3. Trade secrets + customer lists = company gold.

Don't take from others and don't let others take yours.

We must pause in this journey toward building an overwhelmingly successful business with an admonition that may seem obvious to some and completely sail over the heads of others. Most entrepreneurs arrive at the starting line of a new business with a vision for the future and some degree of experience from the past. Often, that experience comes from being employed within a business that was similar, but whose senior management may have missed or deliberately ignored what the entrepreneur sees as a great opportunity.

And most senior and middle level managers will understand when a subordinate comes to them to resign and begin a new business. But all will immediately question whether the new business will compete in any way with their enterprise, and react to the future entrepreneur in either of two very distinct ways based upon those fears.

If the employee who is about to resign is off to conquer the world in a completely new arena, there is almost always the unspoken sigh of relief and a cooperative attitude that flows from the senior manager from that point on in the conversation.

But if the employee is even a little bit reticent to tell of the plan envisioned, the result is the first stage of what could become an outright war between the present employer and a newly separated past employee, sent away that day with an escort out the door.

The same attitudes from past employers can be expected if a past employee resurfaces after a layoff, resignation or after being fired, with a plan for a competitive business. Most employers have all their employees sign non-disclosure and confidentiality agreements to protect the company's trade secrets, customer lists and business plans. Many states recognize the right of a former employee to work, even if in direct competition with a past employer. But that right clearly stops when the entrepreneur uses any trade secret data from the past employer, especially customer lists for contacts and confidential business plans as bases for new businesses.

Anyone can be sued even if without merit, and responding to a suit can be traumatic in many ways – from expenditure of cash and valuable time to emotional drain from worry over a negative outcome, to loss of industry goodwill by an entrepreneur perceived to have stepped over the line.

This is especially true for someone who has sold a business only to surface later to compete in some way with the buyer. Never underestimate the venomous response from such a threat.

So no matter what your circumstance, never, ever be guilty of using trade secret materials or ideas from your past employer, especially customer lists.

4. Vision is everything.

I love absolute statements. And this is one of my favorites. You're at the ignition stage of a new business venture. Of course you have a vision for what that business will do to change the world. And this insight is directed to you in an attempt to stress test that vision and sharpen it further to help insure your success.

Let me address those whose vision may be limited and who will be happy with a successful local dry cleaning enterprise or small restaurant around the corner. Although many of these insights will help you succeed, you are not the target for this epic effort to help entrepreneurs build great businesses that do change the world. Take what you can from these bursts of insight. I wish you well in your endeavors.

For the rest of you who want to change the world, I am with you and happy to offer all the help I can to reinforce your opportunities for success.

To you, let me repeat: vision is everything. A great vision for a new enterprise drives innovation. It serves as the rallying cry for all future employees, investors, customers and even suppliers. It sharpens the understanding of those new to the enterprise and moves them to follow and even to become unpaid advocates for the business.

Think of some of the great visions from the past that did change the world. "Absolutely, positively overnight" made FedEx an indispensible name in supply chain management. "A computer on every desk" made Microsoft a partner in the growth of most every business. You can think of many more, visions expressed so clearly that the enterprise became critical to your own success.

There are other, less dramatic ways to express a vision. "Be the largest supplier of laser toner in North America", or "Make dining into a five star experience."

Years ago, as a panelist at an entrepreneurial seminar, I watched as over fifty aspiring young entrepreneurs filed past a microphone, each tasked with making a thirty second pitch to the panelists of professional investors. About halfway through this painful exercise, one man walked up to the microphone and said, simply, "We move oil through the Internet" and then he moved on. Immediately after the panel presentation, I found that one entrepreneur and began a conversation that led to my investing $100,000 in his vision of a supply chain enterprise based upon perfect knowledge of oil delivery systems, precise timing of delivery and coordination of resources to move oil from source to customer using the Internet as a frictionless tool for communication and coordination.

Although that business ultimately failed, I still speak with that entrepreneur as he uses his experience in a new field, better off as a result of his learning experience. I carry no rancor as a result of the loss, since I bought into the vision, helped as I could with the execution, and came to the realization along with the entrepreneurial team that the number of uncontrollable elements far exceeded those which could be controlled by any third party at that stage of development of the Internet.

We will explore vision in more depth in recognition of its importance to success.

5. Address ten vision tests for success.

A vision must be solid and flexible enough to pass a number of critical tests if it is to guide a business enterprise to greatness. Here in brief are ten tests for a successful vision. Try these on for size, and test yourself for attractiveness to the marketplace, to investors and to history.

Ten tests for a successful vision

1. *Is your market identifiable and accessible?* Test yourself as to whether you can identify the size of your market niche, and

whether you can overcome the many barriers to access customers within your niche.

2. *Where in industry life cycle?* If your vision is for a product or service that fills a need in a mature industry, you may be flying against the prevailing winds as a market shrinks over time, taking your business with it. Conversely, a fast growing industry lifts most all good participants, making excellent companies excel even more and grow even faster, like a small plane flying at 150 knots with a 75 knot tailwind.

3. *How large a total market?* If the total market for your niche is under $100 million per year, it is going to be difficult to build a $50 million business, even if not impossible. If the market is ten times that size, there is probably room for competitors to fight for dominance and still succeed if you are not number one.

4. *Can you dominate that market?* The dominant player in any niche controls pricing for all those under it, and often sets the risk profile for new entrants into the niche if the dominant player's products or services fill the needs of customers at reasonable prices and quality.

5. *Have you created high barriers to entry?* If your business is a "me too" entrant into any market niche, even the smallest success will soon attract competitors that will sap some degree of your potential growth. What can you prove as a barrier to entry for competitors? Is it the advantage of time – years of development ahead of any competitor? A core patent or "thicket" of patents protecting your offering? A strategic relationship with one or more of the largest customers?

6. *Are margins high enough?* Some great ideas just can't make money and ultimately die for lack of profit potential. Profit margins are higher for unique products or services early in

the life of an industry niche, or for products protected by patents that prevent others from undercutting you simply by releasing a cheaper product. High profit margins are a sign of high barriers to entry and attract investors and ultimately good buyers for your business.

7. *Can this business grow to above $50MM?* This is a basic test for investors, separating your business from those with smaller visions. There is nothing wrong with a vision for a smaller enterprise if not in need of professional investors to make it a reality.

8. *Do you have a world-class management team?* The best way to protect against failure is to attract a team with members who have experienced success and failure and can recognize the ways to manage toward success and avoid the pitfalls previously experienced from past failures. From a professional investor's perspective, the team should be able to be flexible, coachable and experienced enough to get a business through breakeven and beyond the next level of outside investment, greatly reducing execution risk.

9. *Can you translate an idea into a compelling product?* Some great ideas just cannot be made into a product at a reasonable enough prices to attract customers. And some attract early adopters but cannot pass into the mass market. Sometimes, an idea is just too early for the available technology to make it attractive. Early cell phones were large bricks that required a large carrying case and cost up to a dollar a minute to use. As technology caught up, allowing miniaturization and light weight, mass adoption drove the price down and allowed the building of infrastructures everywhere to support the use of inexpensive minutes. Do anything you can to develop compelling products or early prototypes as proof of ability to reduce technology risk.

10. *Is there an exit strategy for the investor(s) over time?* There are many professional services businesses that make fine lifestyle opportunities for architects, doctors and dentists. But these types of businesses are not attractive to potential buyers willing to pay a premium for businesses that are worth millions more than their asset value. Building a great business to create wealth for the entrepreneur at exit, means thinking of the exit strategies from the beginning. Who or what type of buyer would be attracted to this business if successful?   Great wealth is made from selling great businesses at immense profit for the entrepreneurs and investors who took the journey.

6. A compelling vision drives innovation.

Companies that innovate new products, services and methods of delivery are the ones that stand out in a crowded business world, especially when attempting to gain recognition beside competitors on the web.

Innovation is valued by our society, by investors and certainly by consumers. It is the focus for state and federal governments worldwide, many finding ways to reward innovators with tax incentives or investors with tax credits to finance innovative new enterprises.

As a keynote speaker, I often start presentations that start with a short history of innovation in the United States, using the twist of examining innovation through the lens of 150 years of cyclic bursts of bubbles, leading to subsequent recessions and depressions. It is not hard to find strands of gold in the carnage left by failed businesses lost when a bubble bursts, such as in 1857, 1902, 1929 and 2001.

Innovators make use of golden strands of opportunity left when the unfinished vision of another cries for completion, or when a genuine new concept changes the very way people think about their lives.

Leonard Kleinrock and a few of his UCLA computer lab students worked to send the first several characters from UCLA to Stanford in 1969 over a direct line established for the test. They were able to send only the "LO" of "LOGON" before recording the very first crash of the Internet. And I'm sure they had no idea what they were fathering with that effort which eventually became ARPANET, and then of course, the Internet itself. They had no mantra, and a limited vision to connect mainframe computers to share academic information.

How many entrepreneurs used that infrastructure to create an expansive vision of what could be? Tim Burners-Lee wanted to use this new infrastructure to create a friendlier web of pages, sharing data like the pages of a massive library of books extending throughout the world. The result was the worldwide web, upon which Mark Andreeson and his crew in Chicago build the Mosiac browser to make this data more available to anyone. Which in turn allowed innovators worldwide to create applications inside a browser, share detailed information previously locked inside libraries and corporations, and ultimately to change the world by making the exchange of information frictionless.

We can look back to Edison, Ford and Bell as great innovators of their time. But perhaps the most impressive invention of recent times is the result of hundreds of people, firms, and institutions, each adding a new brick to the building of the Internet.

Now we have the infrastructure for innovators to create applications with free software on computers used for many purposes simultaneously. And millions of innovators are at work extending the capabilities of the Internet.

What opportunities are next? Perhaps it is the remaking of the world through green technologies, clean technologies, new medical technologies, new home entertainment products, new mobile communications products and services, and more.

Who said that *"Everything that can be invented has been invented?"* Ah yes. That was Charles H. Duell, U.S. Commissioner of Patents in 1899. Oops.

7. Fewer words, greater effect.

I have a business friend, an experienced manager and teacher with a Harvard MBA, whose creativity and intelligence are admired by many. But he dilutes his effectiveness with wordy PowerPoint presentations. It has become a long running joke between us, as I often remind him that most of us have a very limited attention span and ability to recall important points from a presentation.

Note the title and tone of these insights. Short, to the point.

Mark Twain said, "I didn't have time to write a short letter so I wrote a long one instead." He cogently encapsulated the problem.

It is more difficult to reduce your thoughts to a few core sentences, but that is what you should do for maximum effect.

8. Set a realistic goal. When reached, set another.

There's a big difference between your vision for your company, your mission and your goal. Your vision tells the world what you want to be as you contemplate in advance how you will change the world for the better. Your mission merely states who you are and what you do. It is used to limit and sift your opportunities to keep you from using resources for projects outside of your core, your mission.

But your goal is a tangible aiming point, one that should be achievable within several years if you accomplish your progressive steps planned between now and then. You can express it in terms of money, market share, influence or other measure that reflects success. An example: "To be at a $25 million run rate by the end of our fifth year in business." That is measurable and from this you'll be able to look backward to develop a set of steps (strategies) to achieve that goal.

Once achieved, a goal is meant to be overwritten with a newer one, set to even higher standards. If achieved early, celebrate and set another goal earlier than planned.

The good thing about a goal is that it is measurable, and progress toward it can be measured as well. Unlike a mission or even a vision, neither of which may be measured, there is a satisfaction in each step toward achievement. Better yet, your employees and investors will appreciate constant attention to the goal and reports of progress toward it. A goal serves as a rallying point for all associated with your vision.

Make the goal realistic, achievable and public. You'll find others buying into the objective and even creating better ways to achieve it because they are invested in the dream and the measure of that dream – the mutual goal.

9. Map your goal and use your map.

It's time to speak of some sort of business plan. As a professional investor in early stage companies, I have long discounted long, detailed business plans in favor of a concise "executive summary" followed by a believable spreadsheet-based financial forecast projecting three to five years into the future.

Yes, everything does change between drafting that plan and its successful execution. But flying without a map of some kind seems just plain too risky.

I recently joined the board of a company that was growing slowly, running beyond breakeven, but had not approved a plan for the current year, let alone attempted to develop one for the next. So the CEO had one of his own that he did not share, while the CFO had one for internal use that was never shown to the CEO or to the Board. No wonder the Board members wanted to dig in and find who was communicating with whom, and who was in charge of the map to the goal. By the way, there was no goal understood by all or agreed to by anyone. How do you compensate executives and all levels for successful accomplishments if there are no established steps toward the goal? And how do you measure a person's contribution to an unnamed goal?

So if you have not, create a concise map for your enterprise. Start with a reasonable goal, usually expressed as a revenue number some number of years in the near future. Assess your current resources and attempt to calculate the resources needed to accomplish the goal. Do you need to raise money, focus spending upon only core projects that advance the company toward the goal, or bring in new management talent to make it happen? Write these steps down in any form for now. We'll explore a more organized approach in the next insights.

10. Strong strategies + tactics support your goal.

Now we're getting organized. There are many ways to express the roadmap for your enterprise. One of the most popular was used by the U.S. Army late in World War II, and adopted by a number of high profile businesses such as Texas Instruments after the War. The structure combined the listing of the goal with a series of strategies and then tactics, each designed to support each other, each measurable and made public throughout the organization. The technique, "OST" (objective, strategies and tactics), is a very good way to organize your effort to find guideposts and then develop metrics to measure progress.

What is a strategy? It is a medium range process involving senior management and departmental management as well, directing resources in ways that, as accomplished, lead the company toward the goal. A typical small to medium, business finds five sweeping strategies for the current year, many cross-departmental, and some carried over from the previous year's plan and even from years before that. Here are some example strategies from some of my companies over the recent years.

- Expand into at least three new continents through new distribution channels.

- Penetrate the Fortune 500 with at least five active accounts within two years.

- Create a hosted "software as a service" or "on demand" addition to our product line by end of (next) year.

Note that these are expansive "junior" goals that, if achieved, would certainly move the company forward toward a larger financial goal. Yet each is measurable if achieved. In fact, the degree of progress toward achievement can also be achieved, such as "We did establish and do business with two of the five Fortune 50 accounts this year."

Measurement is the key to success. Even at the strategic level. Next we'll look at the last major step in creating an OST plan for an entire organization.

11.   Five strategies + five tactics = one goal

In past insights, we explored the need for a tangible goal and strategies that are measurable as steps toward achievement of the goal.

This insight calls to account tactics to accompany each strategy, and even suggests a number for each.

Tactics support strategies and allow your individual managers and departments to contribute to strategies in measurable ways that are more short term and procedural than are the strategies they support. Tactics change frequently as achieved and may be updated or replaced during a year when achieved, unlike strategies which often span a number of years.

Five tactics to support each strategy seem a fair, even if arbitrary number. Tactics direct each department in very specific ways. Here are several examples of tactics from my recent experience with companies where I serve as board member.

Strategy Three: Expand into at least three new continents through new distribution channels.

1. Sign one distributor by June of this year in each of three major geographic areas. EMEA, Asia, Latin America. Each distributor to be capable of generating $1 million in business by year two.

2. Assign development manager to localize design and oversee needed enhancements to product and support materials for each new territory.

3. Train and transfer technology to each new distributor within 90 days of signing.

4. Assign one corporate employee to support sales and installation efforts by all distributors.

5. Seed demand in each new territory with at least two corporate marketing events in partnership with each distributor.

Note that each of these tactics directly support the strategy, are measurable and assumed to be achievable, bought into by each department effected by the tactic. Note that the strategy calls for cooperation between business development, sales, marketing, product development, installation and support. This is a great way to unify departments that once may have competed for resources toward individual ends, now pointed toward a common goal supported by all levels of management up to the CEO.

In planning, the matrix, "5x5=1" is a good memory tool for management to keep from overreaching with too many strategies and too many tactics.   But it is not written in stone.   And development of these important elements of the plan should be made using all the resources available, from your board of directors to your senior management to departmental management. Getting all to buy into each step may not be easy, but when accomplished, is a powerful and invigorating opportunity to celebrate, then to get to work as a functional unit of the whole.

12. Your budget and forecast light your goal.

Let's spend a few moments defining a sometimes confusing set of terms. A budget should be created each year as a result of a series of negotiations between departmental managers and their superiors through to the CEO, all in support of the next year's tactics previously agreed upon (which in turn support the longer term strategies leading to the next goal beyond).

So a budget sets the limits upon spending for the next year that are negotiated between the players. An important part of the budget is the expected revenue for the coming year, a critical factor in setting hiring and resource expectations for the year.   During the year, if the forecast revenues fall short or are greatly exceeded, it is fair to revise the budget and rethink hiring and resources. Otherwise, it is the expectation of the board of directors of a company that each year's budget be approved in advance and adhered to as long as revenue goals are met.

Note that I used the term "forecast" for revenues for the next year. The term is also used when projecting revenues for succeeding years. The term "forecast" is a bit confusing, because it is also used by some as a measure of expected revenue and expenses to the end of the current year, found by taking actual performance year-to-date and adding best estimates of remaining revenues and expenses for the rest of the year to obtain an expected or "forecast" outcome at yearend. Both uses of the term are common. Just be sure all who participate understand which use of the word is the current one.

The real point here is to create a financial plan to support the strategic plan, marrying them in harmony one with another. Many entrepreneurs are impatient by nature, not the best of detailed planners. Yet, with the assistance of those in support such as the CFO, everyone in management must be aligned in a single direction, reviewed and updated annually as accomplishments, the marketplace, and even the competitive landscape change.

13. Use metrics and dashboard. Act upon variances.

Have you ever driven a car that had no speedometer? I had that thrill when a student at the Richard Petty Stockcar School of Driving recently at a motor speedway in California. With a wide track, angled aggressively at the curves, and being told to hug the wall on the straighaways, there was little reference available to a novice driver as to speed. I followed my instructor's car closely, but still could not tell anything about my speed, so that I could either compensate for lags behind the leader or a test my comfort zone at various points that matched the expectation of my instructor and my own increasing capabilities as a driver. Upon conclusion of eight laps of this, after pulling into the alley and climbing through the window on the driver side (there are no doors in these cars), I was handed a sheet with my timings for each of the eight laps. Only then, after when the information might have been useful, could I see how well I did.

That's how you would feel if you ran your company without a dashboard containing relevant metrics that drive your company. If you cannot relate to this, then you probably have been driving without a speedometer from the start and need to pay particular attention.

Metrics should be created by you and your managers to measure near real time progress for your enterprise. A number of these deemed critical to you and your managers should be combined into a single page on your desktop screen or in printed form and available or circulated as often as daily.   These measures of progress must be fresh and meaningful. Yesterday's sales and returns compared to same day last week and last year for retail businesses;   Units produced and units shipped compared to plan and same period last month for manufacturers; Yesterday's overtime hours by department; Ratio of hours worked to units produced; Backorders unshipped; Customer service calls in cue or unresolved.

You can think of numerous critical measures for your business that must not be ignored, but often are neglected by senior management. It is not bad to manage by walking around, a term that became popular as a result of another of the many business advice books of the '90's. But that method, although good for employee morale, is imprecise as a tool of measurement and should be relegated to a supporting role. Financial information for last month compared to plan and same month last year is certainly relevant, but not part of a dashboard, since there is nothing you can do to fix a problem when numbers are as old as a week, let alone the typical several weeks required to prepare financial statements for review.

Finally, what good is the information contained in a great dashboard if you ignore it? Show that you value the information by acting immediately upon variances, even if only to question the numbers. Everyone down the line will become aware of your attention to their work, your interest in the outcomes and care for their success. And you will drive revenue and better control costs and the customer experience with quick reaction to the variances within critical metrics the best describe your immediate situation.

So we have come to the arbitrary end of business state one – ignition. You have planned for, created and organized a fine business with minimum friction from un-oiled parts. You've hired the best and found ways to measure their workflow that are meaningful to all. Perhaps you did all this with your own capital from savings or from credit card debt. But at some point the growth of your enterprise will be throttled by the need for capital. And you will probably consider external sources for that capital early in the fundraising process. Stage two of *Berkonomics* is set to quickly explore the sources and responsibilities that come from such capital-raising.

Chapter Two. RAISING MONEY

This stage is critical to many businesses and a passing option to others, depending upon the capital efficiency of the enterprise. Some businesses require very little capital and the founder is able to self-finance the enterprise and retain 100% of its ownership and control from ignition through liquidity event (startup through sale). For you who fit that description, nice work. For the rest of us desiring to build large, valuable enterprises quickly, the need for outside capital is high on our list of requirements and even the source for some sleepless nights as we worry over the availability and cost of capital. It is for this group that we explore the implications implicit in raising money for growth.

Before we explore the next insight, it might be useful to list some of the ways in which you can raise money for growth with and without outside investors.

Bootstrapping: This term describes your ability to start a business with little investment and grow it using internally-generated funds. Certainly bootstrapping is a preferred method of funding growth if it does not hold back the speed of growth or hobble the quality of product or service to the extent that better-funded competitors can overtake the business. There is a lot to say about retaining control. You will realize much more from the ultimate sale of your business even if at a considerably lower price than if splitting the proceeds with investors. You will have more control over strategy and execution than with an outside board overseeing planning and performance. But few businesses grow into the sweet spot of $20 million to $30 million in worth to an ultimate buyer without the injection of outside capital.

Friends, family and fools: This term, although pejorative, describes the typical mix of early investors in a small, young growing business. Money from these sources is relatively easy to come by, and most often comes with no strings as to oversight by a formal board composed of these investors and management. However, most often, these funds are solicited by a well-meaning entrepreneur from investors who are not qualified as accredited investors under the law (currently requiring a proved income of $200,000 a year or $1 million in net worth for an individual investor). I've arrived at a significant number of companies that were looking for additional growth capital after a "friends and family" round, and had to "clean up" the cap table more than a few times over the years. Taking this kind of money has a number of pitfalls you should be aware of. It is most common to greatly overprice such a round of financing, valuing the enterprise well above what it may be worth at the moment for friend or related investors who do not have the sophistication or willingness to challenge the valuation. When professional investors look at such overvalued prior investments, they may refuse to become involved with a company, knowing that there will be, at the very least, universal disappointment and anger from prior investors when a new round is priced lower than the earlier friends and family round. Sometimes this money is just too available and the risks seem so far away; so an entrepreneur will take the money and put off the worry over the eventual consequences, all in the hope that no more investment will ever be needed and everyone will be richer for the effort.

Using your bank credit line and credit cards: Even with the credit crunch signaled by the recent recession, many banks will issue business credit cards with a $50,000 limit if the entrepreneur is willing to personally guarantee the balance, and has the net worth to do so. And even with the significant cost of credit card debt, many entrepreneurs aggressively use existing cards to finance a startup. It's an option, even though an expensive one.

"Strategic partner" investors: If you can find a strategic partner willing to invest in your enterprise, consider it a blessing. Whether the partner is a supplier looking to gain a lock on your business as it grows or a customer looking to create a competitive barrier through use of your product, such an investment typically carries fewer restrictions than from a professional investor and less oversight. Better yet, the valuation of your enterprise is often higher than if the same investment were taken from a professional investor. Strategic investors validate a business, by their presence creating the very value they pay for with increased price per share purchased. It is most often a win-win for both you and the strategic partner.

Professional angels: This is the arena where I work and play. This class of investor, once quite disorganized, has become much like the venture capital community, creating a process including due diligence (careful examination of a business before investment), terms of investment that match those of venture capitalists, and a process that often takes months from introduction to investment. Yet, professional angels are usually willing to take active board seats in a young enterprise and act as cost-free consultants to the CEO-entrepreneur, giving freely of their individual and collective years of experience, often in the same industry as the investment target. Do not expect grand valuations of your enterprise from these professional angels. They have been burned too badly during the last decade by overvaluing businesses and finding themselves like friends and family, "stuffed" into a down round of lower valuation when a company takes its next round of financing from the next step, venture capitalists. Professional angels, often organized into groups, usually invest from $100,000 to $1 million in a young enterprise.

Venture, private equity and more: Here we lump a large number investor classes into one. Venture capital comes with a cost, and there are no bargains for the company when taking such an investment. VC's value an enterprise lower than others might at the same stage of investment, always aware of the need to create opportunities for "home run" profits at exit, since over fifty percent of their investments typically are lost when companies die before an opportunity to sell to others. Further, as a class, VC's have not done well for their own investors over the past decade since the bubble burst, making it doubly important to fight for low valuations and high profits at exit. VC's do not even engage in discussion with most of those entrepreneurs seeking capital. By some estimates, 95% of contacts are ignored unless they come as referrals from trusted sources such as known lawyers, accountants or fellow VC's. And just for measure, VC's fund less than 2% of all deals they do investigate. Typical VC investments begin at $2 million and quickly rise to $5 million and above, depending upon the size of the fund and stage of investment. Terms are much more restrictive than from strategic or angel investors, often requiring the entrepreneur to escrow his or her founder stock for a number of years to prevent the founder leaving, and restricting the sale of prior stock without the VC also being allowed to offer a share of its holdings in the same sale.

Private equity investments are available from firms created for this later stage opportunity, but typically are available only for businesses that have achieved revenues well above $50 million. Often private equity investors will want control of the business as well.

Bank lines of credit are often available to businesses that are profitable, most often personally guaranteed by the entrepreneur, but available at a cost in interest less than most any other source. Small Business Association (SBA) federally-guaranteed bank loans are becoming available again after years of limited activity. With some restrictive provisions, these loans are favored by many banks as carrying much less risk than loans without the guarantee.

But it is the outside investor that validates a business, often influencing growth with shared relationships, experienced guidance and providing a gateway to needed resources. There are a few insights that relate to this money resource, and you should know and respect these...

14. Outside investors want liquidity not love.

Taking in angel or venture money requires a setting of an entrepreneur's expectations that may come as a shock at least at first. From the moment such an investor looks seriously at your company, the investor or VC partner is thinking of the end game, the ultimate sale of the company or even of an eventual initial public offering. There is no middle ground. Taking money from these sources involves resetting priorities over time. There is no such thing as a lifestyle business with outside investors. To protect against such an event, almost every professional investor includes a clause in the investment documents which allow the investor to "put" the stock back to the company after five years, requiring the company to pay back the investment plus dividends accrued during the term of the investment. This sword hanging over the company is not often used, but is a constant reminder that an outside investor is serious about getting out, hopefully in less than five years, at a profit, usually from the sale of the company. Many companies find themselves at the five year point completely unprepared for a sale and without the cash resources to carry out such a repurchase of investor stock, making the clause moot.

There are also clauses in many such investor documents that allow the investor to override the founder and force a sale of the company if a proposed sale is attractive to an investor for liquidity, even if the founder feels that there is much more potential if the business is not sold at the present time.

Finally, it is an unfortunate fact that when a company needs money and has not met its original planned targets, the newest investor prices the round at a level below the last or last several rounds of financing, angering and frustrating previous investors who took what they perceive as the greatest risks by investing before the business proved itself. The last money has the first say – in valuation and in sometimes forcing draconian terms that require prior investors to contribute a proportional new investment to retain a semblance of their original rights and avoid dilution or worse yet, involuntary conversion to a lower class of stock. As the years progress with typical VC firms seeing lower returns than expected by their limited partner investors, such terms are more common in secondary rounds of financing, causing a real riff between angel investors and their former close allies, the VCs, with whom they had once coexisted as suppliers of deals at expectedly higher valuations at each state of investment.

So be aware that professional investors are in your company for the eventual large profits at the liquidity event. They are your friends only as long as you meet or exceed planned growth and value. They tolerate you and your management when the numbers are a bit murky but with an explanation that is believable and correctable. They act in their own best interests when things go south. That's just the facts.

15. Raise cash from trusted, close resources first.

This insight follows closely the conclusions from the previous declaration, that professional investors negotiate tough terms, from provisions of control over asset acquisition, eventual sale of the company, future investments, forced co-sale when others attempt to sell their shares and more. And yet, in an earlier insight, we spoke of the problems that come when taking unstructured investments from friends and family. So how does the statement above fit into this sandwich of alternatives?

Trusted, close resources include sophisticated relatives, friends and business associates who know how to structure a deal as a win-win for you and for them, while allowing you to retain control over your vision and execution. Their investment should be structured with the help of a good attorney who understands the mutual goal of maximum leverage of funds with minimum interference in your business decisions.

Remember the admonition that investment from such close sources carries an additional burden for you – to protect your investors and their investment as if they were your alter egos, offering money as if from your own pocket. Such money should never be taken without clear understanding of the terms, whether a loan with a reasonable interest rate and strict repayment terms, or an investment valuing the company at an amount considered reasonable by a third party professional, even if as a sanity check as opposed to an appraisal. This money is personal, an investment in you as much or more than in your company. The degree of care you take increases with the reduced distance between you and your investor.

My very first investment as a professional angel was in a small startup where the entrepreneur's vision fueled my imagination in the audio market niche where I had run a business in an earlier life. I was so enthusiastic that I coached the entrepreneur to approach his mother, who invested $50,000 under the same terms as my investment. A small venture firm and a few more angels rounded out the total investment. As the company grew and became profitable, it became more visible to others in the market niche. Two of us who invested served on the board of the company, advising the first-time entrepreneur with our business and industry experience. Several years later, with the approval of the board end entrepreneur, I was able to engage a very well-known potential acquirer of the business who offered an attractive price for the still-young but successful enterprise. After weeks of negotiation, the entrepreneur suddenly disengaged, claiming that he was no longer interested in a sale of his company. The rest of us were shocked and disappointed that after weeks of work and a fair price, we were left with nothing but to follow his lead and disengage. Shortly thereafter, in a board meeting, I brought up the issue of starting to pay board members for service in cash or in stock options, typical for outside board members but rarely for investors. The entrepreneur was angry, abusive, in his negative reaction to even bringing the issue to the board for a discussion. Five years had passed from my original investment in what I now clearly perceived as investment into a lifestyle business, one where the entrepreneur had no interest in selling or sharing. I resigned from the board on the spot and negotiated a sale of my stock to the entrepreneur at five times the earlier investment, a fair return for both, since the company was by then worth much more. It is now years later, and his mother along with other early investors are still in the passive game, not likely to see liquidity from this mistaken investment in an entrepreneur unwilling to take money in exchange for the eventual promise of liquidity.

Why tell this story at all? Mother is surely satisfied as a passive investor who probably would have given her son the money without structure. The other investors are probably in the unhappy never land of not being able to see liquidity after a decade and unable to write off the investment as a loss for tax purposes.   This story would probably have ended in a lawsuit if a larger professional investor had been involved, since the entrepreneur did not follow the rules and seems to have no desire to do so.

Trust works both ways. Take money from close resources, but treat it as if the responsibility is even greater to protect the investors and their money than from a professional.   These investors trust that you will do the right thing for them if at all able.

16. Money comes smart or dumb. Find Smart.

This statement could be considered controversial. We have previously made the case that professional investors demand more in the form of restrictive covenants and lower valuations. Now we explore the other side of that coin.   Professional investors usually bring "smart money" to the table, defined as money that comes along with good advice and great relationships for corporate growth. Often, that money is worth more than the cash invested, because the investors who often become members of the board, bring a wealth of experience, insight, relationships and deeper pockets to the table.

I serve on the boards of several companies with just such VC talent at the table, partners in firms that made subsequent investments in companies where I either made early investments or led a group of fellow investors in early rounds of finance. Each of these companies needed more cash than professional angel investors were willing or able to provide, and we turned to the venture community for larger investments.

Attracting a VC investment means finding a partner in a VC firm who is willing to champion your opportunity before his partnership and then represent his firm with a seat on the board once the investment is made. In a number of cases, these VC partners have made the difference between success and failure or at least growth vs. stagnation. These VC partners have relationships with later stage investors further up the food chain, with service providers, with potential "C" level senior managers, and with other CEO's with great timely advice or partnering opportunities. In one such recent case, the angels were tapped out at $6 million invested, an amount far above their usual taste, but for a company with a billion dollar potential. The VC's that subsequently invested $18 million to date are looking for the billion dollar valuation someday, well beyond what angel investors usually are able to project from their own resources. Whether this business and entrepreneur make it to the rare billion dollar club or not, without the VC guidance there would have been little opportunity to even dream of such a goal. There is no question that the company took smart money and leveraged it for maximum growth, using the money, guidance, contacts and more from these large VC investors.

So now we have explored the early stages of formation and finance. It is time to turn to tuning the business and its strategic plan to exploit its maximum potential, finding the ideal niche for a company and its core competency.

Chapter Three. FINDING YOUR NICHE

Here we speak of homework, constantly testing the market and competition and fine tuning the business strategies to compete in an ever-changing world.

17. Market knowledge comes first.

Know your market and competition, or don't spend a dime on anything else.

I have stated previously that I love absolutes – statements with no wiggle room for gray-area responses. Well, here is one of those, and it deals with market research first and foremost.

Let me tell you a short story at my own expense. In 1994, (I know a long time ago), I invested over a million dollars into a company whose entrepreneurs had a vision that I bought into for many reasons, not the least of which was that I had industry experience and understood the need. The first of a number of advanced products was a unique cell phone for hotel rooms, connected through a special "switch" in the hotel's telephone room that was able to detect when a call was coming to the guest room phone and simultaneously ring the cell phone assigned to that room, no matter where it was at the moment. A tent card beside the fully-charged phone greeted the guest entering the room for the first time, inviting the guest to pocket the cell phone for the duration of his stay. The phone could be used for receiving incoming calls when in the restaurant, on the golf course or anywhere. The guest could even make room-to-room or concierge calls as if dialing from the room itself. These systems were not cheap as you might guess. But four and five star hotels loved the concept, which included redirecting outgoing calls from the cell phone by the guest to be sent through the hotel's land line switch, making the hotel a miniature phone company with its attendant profits.

Here's where some intelligent market research might have saved the company and my investment. Fast forward several years to 1996. Hotels were installing the system; guests were satisfied and the company was growing. There was even talk of some phone companies using the patented system for serving communities of guests, not just from a single hotel. Back to 1996. That year, some of you will recall, the first digital cell phones were released to the market, smaller, cheaper and priced with roaming plans that made it no premium cost to carry these digital phones to cities far from home. Overnight, guest use of the room cell phones dried up and hotels were left with expensive switches, phones and chargers unused. Soon the company was drifting toward bankruptcy as the leases for the systems expired, one by one.

I guarantee that there were tens of thousands of people in the country who knew long beforehand of the imminent arrival of the digital cell phone and could predict its effect upon usage, especially roaming use. And yet the company was blindsided as it continued to invest in switch and specialized analog phone hardware, soon to be instantly obsolete. Merely adapting the switches to new digital phones would not work, since guests no longer needed the service itself, being instantly self-sufficient. People no longer called guests in their rooms but directly to their cell phones, even when the guests were on the road.

In this case, the competition was not from a company but a new technology. In most cases, it is the competitor with a better product, lower price, faster service, better reputation that is the threat.

When I listen to a pitch from an enthusiastic entrepreneur or read the summary of a business plan, one of the first questions I ask is about the strength of the competition.   Surprisingly, many entrepreneurs immediately respond. "There is no competition."   Now, there is a statement even Alexander Graham Bell could not make about the telephone (which he pitched to his investors as a device to aid the deaf). Bell's competition was the written message, doing nothing, the telegraph and old fashioned word of mouth. To say "there is no competition" is always the most red of all flags to an investor. For most brilliant new ideas and business plans, the competition is merely to do nothing. That response is quite different than one where competitors have paved the way and existing customers prove through use that the product or service is valued.

So I lost over a million for lack of market research. Bell was lucky, but the pace of technology was so much slower then. Just to make a well-earned point now that you have heard my story, know your market and competition or don't spend a dime on anything else. Oh, how I wish I had taken my own advice.

18. Don't rest until you test.

So you have a great new product or service that you and your associates love. Early adopters should climb all over each other for a look. But what have you done to test the concept against the realities of the marketplace?   Have you developed a prototype, alternate pricing schemes, even a PowerPoint mockup to show to potential buyers? I would be very, very nervous without testing the product in the market as early as possible, ready to make changes and enhancements before committing to production and release.

Even with a perfect product, is the market ready for this? Will you have to be both the evangelist for the product and for its marketplace as well? Few early stage companies have the resources to do both.

There are formal focus group organizations to help you, or you can attempt to test the market yourself by calling together a variety of potential users and asking a third party to facilitate a meeting where the product is exposed to the group and a conversation freely formed allowing the participants to agree with the premise or reject the product as useless to them, all without personalities getting in the way.

No matter how you plan to test, make that plan an integral part of the development cycle, as early as possible so changes will not be costly. Do NOT rest until you test.

19. Everything changes from concept to release.

You can take this as a rule, not an exception. You'll recognize the truism, *"No battle plan ever survives contact with the enemy"* first stated by German Field Marshall Helmuth Karl Bernhard Graf von Moltke in the 19th century. This variant of the "battle plan" truism is important to internalize. A product at the concept stage contains feature-functionality that customers may not want or be willing to pay for, or which just might not work well enough for release to the public.

You may recall that Microsoft planned a new file system for Vista, but pulled the file system from the product before release, and has not released the WinFS file system yet as of this writing, years later. It is interesting to note that not many of us even remember this "feature" let alone miss it.

Plan for change; sometimes at the last minute. Allow for the cost and extra time for tweaks to the product or service. Make the first release a limited, controlled one, so that changes and corrections can be made much more easily than if a general release all at once.

And how do we protect ourselves against surprises that relate to feature-functionality as opposed to product quality upon release? Early contact exposing friendly close customers to the product are critical to the development staff, marketing and even to the customer that feels closer to your enterprise as a result of the special treatment. This is not to state that the customer tests a new product before we do internally, although many of us are surely guilty of that error.

Back when I was developing early systems for the hotel industry, with the full cooperation of the owner and managers of a hotel in Tulsa, Oklahoma, I would fly in from Los Angeles on Friday evenings, install new releases that night and make fixes on the fly in a real 24 hour environment. Sunday afternoon, just about departure time for my scheduled flight, the hotel manager would drive me to the airport barely in time to make the returning flight. My excitement in having developed so many new and "somewhat tested" features over a sleepless weekend was exceeded only by the enthusiasm of the entire hotel staff for the new and wonderful capabilities left behind after the magic weekend of non-stop programming. These trips were so common and their aftermath so predictable (a late night emergency repair call waiting for me at home upon return Sunday evening) that the hotel owner created a mantra that stuck with me and caused quite a laugh at my expense for years. He would be sure to remind his staff, shaking my hand goodbye as I left in a hurry to catch that Sunday evening flight: "Wheels up, system down." I am not advocating such brazen behavior today. "Cowboy coding" is no longer common or permissible in the computer software industry, especially for enterprise systems. But those were the days.

20. Find your "teacher customer."

Your customers know what they want more than you do. Find one to teach you.

This insight came from personal experience and from a good friend who advanced the notion of the "teacher-customer" years ago. I internalized this phrase, recalling the many times I had partnered with customers to design new feature-functionality into my hotel computer system back when such systems were brand new to the industry. It was an ideal partnership between my growing company, as it approached one hundred employees on the way to almost two hundred fifty, and selected special customers anxious and willing to spend time telling us of their pain points. Together we would work out solutions in the form of new functions, new controls, new reports, and new safeguards. The customer would be the first to receive the new functionality in a new release. At the annual user conference, I would often make sure the entire user community present knew of these extraordinary collaborations by naming the teacher-customers in the presence of their contemporaries. Sometimes the audience would cheer one of their own, knowing that everyone benefited from the extra time and effort spent teaching their vendor the needs of the industry not yet addressed by competitors or by our firm to date.

This is not to bend this insight into a claim that a company should wait to develop new, groundbreaking products and services until a customer asks for them. If that were the ideal mode, many game-changing concepts would never have made it to market, including Fred Smith's FedEx, first explained to a college professor in a paper returned with a C+ grade and the professorial comment that the idea was "good but impractical".

Even if you are an expert in an industry segment, partnering with one of those rare, willing teacher-customers during the design stage for your proposed product or service is empowering and fruitful for both parties.

All companies whether service or product-oriented must fight to gain and maintain quality of product, or fall to the bottom of the competitive heap. We have explored feature-functionality. Now it is time to focus upon stage four in our exploration of insights, product quality and its effects upon the organization.

Chapter Four. The FIGHT FOR QUALITY

21. Greatly exceed early customer expectations.

First customers are critical. Greatly exceed expectations at all costs.

There is so much history behind this insight, and so many stories that illustrate this point. Your first customers for any product or service form your reference base, the important group of allies that your marketing and sales people rely upon when attempting to create buzz and make a mass market for a new product. If you've been involved in the launch stage of any product in the past, you should recognize the overwhelming feeling of panic when initial customers make first contact with complaints about quality, functionality, speed of service or other critical part of the new release.

The best advice I can give is to allocate all of your resources to supporting the roll-out of a new product, at least for a short period. Respond immediately to every question and complaint. Capture every compliment and ask if you can use it for marketing purposes. If the product or service is especially complex or expensive, send someone from sales or marketing or even R&D to the customer location at the moment of first use.

Of course most of us have limited resources for such overwhelming support of a new offering. So make the first release a limited one, sized so you can support it with existing resources, even if that means releasing it to only three carefully chosen customers at first.

And I am serious about the "...at all costs" admonition in this insight. If you must provide a free backup unit, personal on-sight service for a month, your personal cell phone number for the customer CEO, or any number of unexpected offers of superior service and accountability to those first customers, do just that. Make your customer a partner in the process. Send flowers to the staff in the department using the product for the first time if appropriate. Call the customer CEO and thank him for helping launch a product so very important to your success.

The result of doing this right will be to blunt criticism, reinforce compliments and provide a solid user base to build upon. And the alternative is a lost opportunity to shine, perhaps a first wave of negative public reviews that post and report across the Internet, and a loss of reputation and goodwill that will take years to overcome.

I don't know about you, but I would much prefer to spend dollars reinforcing a great first customer's experience than fighting fires in the marketplace after seeing negative reviews. Make sure your entire staff buys into this mantra. "These first customers are critical. You are personally empowered to do everything possible to exceed their expectations."

22. Wasted time is money lost.

There is a relationship between time and money that is more complex than most managers think. Fixed overhead for salaries, rent, equipment leases and more make up the majority of the "burn rate" (monthly expenses) for most companies. Since this number is budgeted and pre-authorized, managers tend to focus upon other things such as sales, marketing and product development issues.

There is an art to efficient management of a process, whether that is the process of bringing a product to market from R&D to production or developing a new product's launch program. What most managers miss is that every month cut from the time it takes to perform such tasks cuts the cost by the value of a month's worth of fixed overhead or burn. Although young companies rarely measure profitability this repeatedly, more mature companies usually can bring from five to ten percent of revenues to the bottom line in the form of net profit. Ignoring cost of product for a moment to make a point, saving a month's fixed overhead by making processes more efficient, could easily double profits for the year.

That relationship between fixed overhead and production time is as critical as any other factor in success of a young company. Many of the start-ups my various angel funds have financed died a slow death, not because of poor concept but because of poor execution, wasting fixed overhead and draining the final resources from the company coffers.

In the technology sector where I most often play, extended unplanned software development cycles account for the majority of these corporate failures. We often accept that development schedules for young companies are almost always too optimistic. But we investors often allow too little slack in our estimates as well. The great majority of young companies developing complex products such as semiconductor-based products, new software-based systems and technologies based upon new processes greatly underestimate the time needed to bring the product to marketable condition. So the CEO comes back "to the well", asking for more money from the investors to complete the project. It is not a strong bargaining position for the CEO to ask for money to complete a product promised for completion with the previous round of funding. And professional investors often penalize the company with lower-priced down rounds or expensive loans as a result.

I have one story that remains as vivid in my mind as when it happened several years ago. Helping the founder create a company and build a much-needed product in an industry I knew very well, I served as chairman for the newly formed company, and along with my several rounds of early investment, led rounds of other angel investors in what I knew as a successful opportunity to fill a need in an industry I understood.

The company grew to be well known in this limited niche and was operating at slightly above breakeven, when the Board and CEO decided to seek venture investment from what we hoped would be a first tier VC firm in Silicon Valley. And we were able to secure that investment along with a partner from that firm joining our board. It did not take long for the partner to become impatient with the relatively small size of the opportunity. Dreaming of a company many times the size, he led the board to approve a complete reversal of course, even stating that the company should ignore the existing market niche completely and redesign the product for the broad Fortune 500 corporate market. Every one of us on the board expressed our concern that the time to make these product changes and position for the new, broader market, would eat away all of the company's capital. Promising the full weight of his VC firm's resources, the board voted to make the change against the best judgment of those of us who knew the original market niche so well and thought that there was growth to spare in that niche alone.

So the company turned the ship, slowly it seemed, as R&D worked to develop an appropriate product using the base of the original design. Time slipped; fixed overhead continued. And exactly as you'd expect, there came the time when the company ran out of money as it ignored its original market. Surprise. Since the company slipped in its R&D schedule, the partners of the VC firm voted to not add new money to the company for the project. Not long after, the company was sold in a "fire sale" amounting to slightly less than the debt on the books. All investors, including the VC firm, lost everything. Do you remember a previous insight, that "the last money in has the first say"? That is what happened within the dynamic of the board, and the result is that the board was completely at the mercy of the "last money" VC to save the company in the end. Yes, there were other issues such as a protracted patent rights fight that drained cash, but the largest problem, inefficient use of R&D time burning fixed overhead, led to the demise of the company. Lots of good jobs were lost and many investors including myself were left with the question. "Why did the company abandon a profitable market, even if it could not generate $100 million a year in revenues?"

We will revisit the relationship between time and money again in future insights.

23. Haste makes waste; but to lag is to sag.

Here we examine the relationship between time, quality and competitiveness. If you are getting the impression from these many insights that complex relationships cause simple problems, you are right.

We have heard the "haste makes waste" ditty since childhood. There is little need to reinforce the obvious. On a larger scale, there are epoch stories of giant companies eating massive losses in a recall of product, often based upon limited testing before release.

A marginal example was the Intel release of the Pentium Pro and new Pentium II processor to rave reviews – until a math professor found an obscure error in the chip's code that made a rare floating point calculation error. Posting that finding on the Internet, quickly Intel found itself defending against fears by others using the processor for math work that the processor could not be relied upon. Intel rushed to fix the bug and offered to replace the processor to anyone requesting such a replacement. At a cost of millions and a reputational hit, Intel recovered. The lesson here is a bit obscure, since it is not clear whether the kind of testing then common in processor design would have surfaced the error. It is quite clear that such an error would be found immediately today based upon changes in testing procedures made by all processor manufacturers after that event.

The waste from haste in this example was in not pre-thinking of enough testing scenarios for a new product. There is always a trade-off between cost for testing, time to market and risk of problems.

Perhaps better examples to point to are easy to find in the toy industry, where recalls because of small parts that could be swallowed by infants or lead-based paint or flammable components make the news on a regular basis.

And the other side of this coin, "To lag is to snag", addresses the two issues of loss to the competition because of delays in release of a new product, and burning of fixed overhead while products are redesigned.

It becomes obvious then that there must be a balance somewhere between rushed release and too much rigor in pre-release planning and testing. Perhaps that balance can be measured in estimating what a company could endure in lost overhead and hits to reputation before becoming crippled and unable to recover. With that measure based upon pure estimates, the balance point changes between companies, with the largest, most profitable companies able to suffer the most risk as to resources, and the smallest suffering by far the most when measuring reputation.

24. No second chance to create first quality.

Let me illustrate this insight with a personal story. As my enterprise computer software company which produced innovative lodging systems for hotels and resorts grew quickly, we found ourselves straining to keep up with the hiring and training of good customer support representatives, a critical part of the equation then and still so today in the 24 hour environment of hotel front desk operations. If a front desk clerk called support at 11.00 PM in the evening, it usually meant that there were guests lined up waiting to check in, anxious to pass beyond this necessary but inconvenient bottleneck between a tiring plane ride and a comfortable bed. The result would be very frustrated clerks facing angry guests if the wait were to be long. It was simply not acceptable to be backed up in customer service, forcing either a ten minute wait or a call back from support.

It took several months to hire and train enough new support reps to keep up with the rapid growth of our company. But the problem was solved, and response times returned to "immediate" for at least this class of customer call. There was no wait, and the quality of response was rated as "excellent" by callers later surveyed. But "There's the rub" (the snag) wrote Shakespeare in *Hamlet.* It took two long years for the company to fully recover its lost reputation after the actual problem was fixed to the satisfaction of all. Aided by salespeople from competitors and long memories from unhappy customers, the myth of continued quality problems in customer support bounced around the industry for those years, until finally good press, great experiences and a marketing campaign together overwhelmed bad memories to put this issue to bed.

If the problems had been in product stability and customer service together at the same moment, there might not have been enough time and resources to recover. There are plenty of young companies that died trying to recover from such a combination.

Your reputation hinges upon delivering a quality product at the moment of release, and maintaining product quality throughout its life. The smaller the company, the more is at stake. There are fewer resources and much less of a reserve of good will among the customer base to absorb a problem release or in the example above, inability to fill the void in customer service created by rapid growth.

25. Know and avoid Time Bankruptcy.

Time bankruptcy results from the deliberate over-commitment of core resources.

I created the term "time bankruptcy" almost thirty years ago when the computer software business was young, and I was a software developer building a young company based upon quality first. Asked to speak at a number of software industry events, I found my voice and immediate audience understanding as I described variants of the following problem to my audience. The insight became clearer as I was hired again and again to pick up the pieces of failed programming efforts by other software companies in this then young industry.

A developer would take on a new customer, customize programs as needed, and install perhaps an 80% completed system upon the customer's brand new minicomputer system. The customer would pay for all or at least 90% of the system, perhaps holding back a retainer awaiting completion. Burning through the payment and needing more to cover fixed overhead, the developer would do the same for the next 80% customer, moving on to the third. About that time, the first would call asking for completion of programming or training, firmly but politely. The fourth installation was interrupted as the first customer suggested that he would stop giving glowing recommendations for the vendor, insisting upon a completion date, while the second customer interrupted with its first call for completion. By the fifth or sixth *(who keeps count for these stories?)*, the first threatens suit, the second becomes demanding and the third makes that expected call for a completion date. So the vendor stops work on the newest installation to complete earlier installations. Revenues dry up while overhead continues to burn though the developer's pockets. It's a classic case of time bankruptcy. The developer deliberately overcommitted his prime or core resources (in this case his personal time) leading to a loss of income and reputation that it could not recover.

The same story could be constructed for any company selecting a limited number of test customers for a new product. Select too many, and pay too little attention to each. Commit all of your core resources to solving the resulting problem, and new work stops. Time bankruptcy. Not a pretty sight, and completely avoidable.

Be aware of this trap. No-one but yourself can be blamed for allowing core resources to be overcommitted, even if by subordinates. That's because you now know the term and the impact of such an error in judgment, and understand that the simple but important remedy is to slow the commitment of those most critical resources to the front lines.

We have arrived at the fifth stage of our examination of insights that impact your business and affect your chances of survival or success. At some point you'll have discovered that you can't do it all alone, whether that is performing a process or managing a growing enterprise. In this stage, we will explore the art and science of hiring, firing, incentive payment and more.

Chapter Five. DEPENDING UPON OTHERS

There comes a time when businesses outgrow the original span of control of the entrepreneur. This critical period is a test of the entrepreneur's desire and ability to delegate, after successfully hiring the best of candidates to fill needed slots in the infrastructure. This stage typically occurs first at about twenty employees or $3 million in revenues for a services or software company. Later, we'll dissect this $3 million dollar phenomenon separately.

But for now, let me digress to the story of my first hiring decision for my first company, years ago. At that time I was managing a small and growing phonograph record manufacturing business (I told you it was awhile ago) using independent contractors for both content and production. I built this business through my high school and college years. Soon after graduating from college, I was making a good living and enjoying growth and freedom managing the enterprise.

It occurred to me that I had come to a fork in my career. I could continue with the status quo, making a good living, or I could reinvest virtually all of my profit into my first hire, an assistant that would free me from the day-to-day management tasks, allowing me to recruit more business (content) and build a real enterprise. This was a tough decision at that time. Comfort, or risk-it-all? On a Friday evening, I got into my car and drove from my office in the Los Angeles area all the way to Ensenada, Mexico, checking into a remote beach hotel. Early the next morning I found a large rock at the shoreline, climbed it, and sat there for hours contemplating my future. Hire for growth, or grow slowly and comfortably? Well, the decision was what you expected. I did hire my first employee, leveraging her organizational skills to grow quickly enough to continue hiring as growth accelerated. The company reached fifty employees at the point where I sold my interest and moved into the computer programming business at what turned out to be just the right time. But I'll not forget the overwhelming weight of that early decision, compared to the many much more expensive decisions made in subsequent years. I was for the first time dependent upon the work of others. And I had made a successful hiring decision, lucky for me.

As years passed, a number of hiring insights became clear as I made mistakes and had successes, and watched other entrepreneurs struggle with similar choices and opportunities. Let me share some of those insights.

26. Hire each as if your success depends upon it.

Provide incentives for success.

Many of us go through the motions of hiring to fill a position, trying to use our intuition and skills to find the best candidate for the job. Sometimes we use consultants or recruiters; many times we use internal talent to fill most positions.

And over the years, we students of business success have learned that there is a science to the hiring process that continues through the life of an employee's tenure with the company. Bradford Smart captured this succinctly in his book, *Topgrading*. His thesis is that "A" players amount only to the top ten percent of the talent pool at any given time, and that your job is to find, recruit and retain only "A" players to make a successful business. It is hard to argue with that. What is hard to find, is the rare CEO that makes the process of hiring top recruits such a priority that he or she spends personal time deeply involved in the specification, resumé review, interview and selection of top employees. Most of us are "far too busy" to do all of that. And yet, aside from managing the vision of the enterprise, the most important job of a CEO is to find, recruit and make productive "A" players for the team.

As an investor and board member for numerous companies, it is increasingly easy for me to quickly evaluate the quality of senior team members in an organization as I probe for strengths and weaknesses in the enterprise. Teams where the CEO is comfortable enough to delegate to "A" players and manage the strategies for growth stand out as rare and powerful. Conversely, it takes very little for a CEO to derail what could be a great team and company, by ignoring the details involved in finding the right talent for each senior position, and by failing to communicate the strategies and empower the team to execute.

A successful hire is not just the responsibility of the recruiter and manager to whom the recruit will report. Many companies require that finalist candidates be interviewed by a number of contemporaries, good employees who fill similar level positions. Some even encourage interviews with those the candidate would manage. Agreement among the interviewers becomes an empowering experience for those conducting the interviews and agreeing to the decision to hire, and paves the way for a quicker assimilation of the new employee into the organization whose cohorts are already prepared to receive and encourage the new hire. This is not an inexpensive process when considering the cost in time and productivity of the interviewers. But finding "A" players is not an easy job, requiring a stretch of resources at each stage of the process.

Earlier, we explored strategic planning within the enterprise. We spoke of developing strategies and tactics that are measurable for each department. Now is a good time to complete that chain by suggesting that paying significant incentive compensation to the people empowered to execute those strategies and tactics is critical to the success of the plan as well as to the organization. Aligning everyone toward the same goal and using the practice of rewarding for achievement of milestones defined by the tactics from planning, makes for a great business, managed by a leader who understands the process.

What makes a great leader great? Of course, it's great execution by great employees acting as a unit in the best interests of the enterprise. No-one can do this alone. No CEO can do this with "B" players or less.

27. Fire fast, not last.

Here is one that takes a real leap for a younger manger or CEO to believe. After hiring someone with all of the attendant enthusiasm followed by the training and learning curve, if an employee shows signs of weakness in the job or problems dealing with contemporaries, it is the natural tendency for most of us to go first into coaching mode, and reset the observation clock to see if our excellent coaching does the job. A month or so later, when no apparent change has been noticed, we may move from coaching to a polite warning and maybe even the dreaded note-to-file. Another month, and the probability of a decision to separate becomes obvious and the move initiated. Lawyers will tell you that this progressive chain of moves is good for the company, protecting against lawsuits by a disgruntled former employee.

But surprisingly, in post-exit interviews after emotions have dissipated, most former employees (who were handled respectfully during the separation process) and most all managers will agree that the move should have been made sooner. The former employee will often state that he or she was at least somewhat unhappy in the job, knowing that the fit was not as good as it should be. The manager will most often admit that he did not move aggressively, following his best judgment in coaching the employee toward separation much earlier.

Firing fast in most every case is best for everyone, as opposed to long, drawn out sessions and stressful employee periods of waiting for a verdict in between sessions. It does sound counterintuitive. But I would believe the post-exit interviews. Why not conduct your own survey of fellow executives and managers and see what they think. If they agree, you should recalibrate your expectations and act sooner, all with the important caveat that employees must always be treated with respect, and there are many times when documentation to file is a required protection for the company against possible lawsuits, especially by protected classes of employees.

28. Equity is the currency of early stage businesses.

The truth of this statement may be obvious, but the execution of a good incentive program using equity is often mismanaged, damaging the corporate capitalization structure and even affecting the outcome of subsequent investment into the company.

First, a brand new enterprise is often formed from the efforts of several "partners", each with an expertise valued by the others. Equity is divided between the founders and the business begun. Although this insight does not address this point of ignition, we should note in passing that things always change over time, and formerly strong founder-contributors can become a drag upon a business or lose interest if the enterprise is not quickly successful. To protect against this, there must be some document in place from the beginning that clearly states the expectation of each founder as to contribution of time and resources to the enterprise. The document should also contain clear buy-sell clauses, forcing any sale of shares to first be offered to the corporate treasury, then to the other founders in proportion to their holdings, and then if no interest, to outside investors. It should contain a mandatory sale clause in the event of separation of a founder, so that a major owner who is passive in the enterprise cannot easily vote against measures other active founders endorse.

The real insight here is that stock options or phantom stock are the tools of early stage businesses used to attract great talent when there is not enough cash to pay market rates. There are some rules. First you must create a stock option plan using your attorney, which must be registered in many states as a security offering. (The fee for registration is well under $100, so this is not an issue.) Options are usually best with "C" corporations, but granting options for either LLC's or "S" corporations are not a real problem.

Most early stage companies make the mistake of making option grants to new hires at all levels that are too aggressive and distort the capital structure of the company to a degree that damages future professional investment. Let me try to advance a few rules of thumb to help guide you here. An option plan should carve out an addition of about 15% of the "fully diluted" shares. If there are 85,000 shares issued to the founders, then a plan calling for 15,000 shares in a pool reserved for future hires is appropriate, making the fully diluted shares 100,000. The board must approve the plan including this number, and shareholders must approve the plan as well. Each grant to new or existing employees must be approved by the board before issue.

The price per share for option grants is also an important consideration. IRS rule 409a specifically calls for an appraisal of the value of the corporation's stock current to within a year of any grants of options, although there is an exclusion for early stage businesses in which expert members of the organization or board may make such an appraisal if they qualify according to the exemption. It there is only one class of stock, the same as the founders, and the appraisal of the single class of shares yields, say $2.00 a share, then options must be priced at that amount. In other words, you cannot create bargain options at below "market rates." If you have a preferred class of stock with special protections, that class of shares will be valued at a price higher than the founder common shares, allowing stock options to carry a lower price per share than preferred investors may have paid. This is important because high quality candidates should be induced to consider coming aboard at lower than market salaries using the tool of "cheap" options, properly priced.

What percentage of the total company shares should be reserved for what specific job titles? Inducing a new CEO to come aboard usually means creation of a stock option package of 5-8%. That size of grant would take much or most of the option pool. A vice president, or CxO candidate, typically is offered between 1% and 1.5%. Director level employees are typically granted ½%. All other grants usually are much lower, allowing for the typical 15% pool to last for quite awhile in most companies.

We will cover board members and advisory board members at a later time.

Options typically are earned over time, which we call vesting. If a grant of 10,000 shares is made on January First, typically there is a four year vesting period in which the employee earns the right to exercise (buy) $1/48^{th}$ of the shares each month. Many plans also call for a one year "cliff" in which an employee who is separated from the company before a year is unable to exercise even the shares which would have been vested at that point.

There is an important consideration that will become an issue with sophisticated candidates for VP and above. We call these "trigger" provisions, in which selected options negotiated for a select group of senior managers, fully vest to 100% upon any change of control. This provision allows these select individuals to perhaps profit handsomely in an acquisition by being able to exercise their options in full at the time of sale. The negative side of this is that the buyer may not want to so enrich these managers that they may not be willing to come aboard the buyer's organization, even if the existing options are replaced with options from the buyer company.

If all of this seems a bit overwhelming, we have just scratched the surface of option plans and incentive compensation. This is an area of expertise that a CEO is required to quickly learn and carefully manage with the help of the corporate attorney and the board.

29. Align incentives with your goals.

And be generous to your high achievers.

Recently I was asked to review an offer letter for a senior director of business development. The CEO was concerned that he was offering far too much in the form of incentive compensation, with bonuses that could greatly exceed the base salary if all of the bonus items were achieved. I asked the CEO to imagine what the company would look like if all of those bonus-expensive items were completely achieved in one year. Upon reflection, he stated that revenues could double the following year, and that the company's reputation among larger customers would be so greatly enhanced that the company could become the leader in its niche. My obvious retort: "Then why not offer this candidate the moon if he can achieve this?" The offer was sent and the CEO much happier, dreaming of the possibilities, not the incremental cost.

I love to point out that my top several sales people were making more than anyone else in the company, including their boss. These outstanding achievers worked for salaries below those of their engineering peers, and had to put it all on the line every day to earn their keep, let alone excel.

The best way to encourage alignment between your managers and the company's goals is to create a bonus plan for each, with its payments made based upon the key performance indicators established for them and for their areas of responsibility, all in turn based upon the tactics and strategies contained in the company's strategic plan.

It is amazing how few company CEOs grasp the concept that executives and managers should be compensated not just for doing their named job, but for exceeding expectations while advancing the corporate goals. To align everyone in the organization in exactly the same direction is a task, one that is a powerful driver for growth. People should be compensated well for such outstanding contributions.

What is the general rule for such a bonus plan? Provide no more than five key performance indicators derived from the strategic plan and fitted to the specific job of the manager. Set time-based goals for each. Provide bonus opportunities that add to approximately 50% of the base salary if all are achieved within the year. Meet and measure progress truthfully each quarter. Perhaps pay a portion of the bonus upon completion of these meetings. Do not make the usual mistake of ignoring or passing on the progress of any of these items by just paying a part of the bonus at yearend because no-one carefully reviewed progress, or because circumstances changed and the bonus item could not be completed as written.

Incentives are powerful tools when used well and reviewed often. They are a major part of a good manager's work and should be treated as such by the CEO and all senior managers.

30. Cash is only one measure of employee happiness.

In 1981, Herb Cohen wrote and published *"You Can Negotiate Anything"*, an excellent guide to great negotiating. I've read and reread the book a number of times and find myself using the techniques often in many areas of my life. One of his lessons remains clearly on my mind and is a variant of the old "You name the price and I'll name the terms" challenge that works so well in negotiation.

Cohen sets up an example where a senior position job candidate is stuck on a salary twice as high as the CEO is willing to pay, leading to a standoff between the two. Cohen goes on to point to twenty five non-cash items that the CEO could have used to narrow and eliminate the gap, many of them untaxed perks worth more than face value because of the employee's tax savings. They include an expense account, company car, profit sharing, 401k contributions, medical coverage for dependents, free life insurance, educational payments, extra vacation, relocation expenses, paid trips to industry association meetings, or a small override on revenue from new products developed under the candidate's watch.

One of the items on Cohen's list of twenty five was stock options. That of course jumps to the top of the list for young, fast growing technology companies.   Many skilled, experienced executives have jumped from mature companies to more risky positions in smaller, fast growing enterprises primarily for the options. In a previous insight, we explored the common percentage of a company's fully diluted stock that is often granted in the form of options for new employees. (See insight 28.)

Many an executive has made much more than any cash compensation from exercise of "in the money" options after taking the leap to a smaller, fast growing company, attracted by just this form of incentive compensation. When used in combination with several of the twenty five additional non-cash forms suggested by Cohen, salary alone does not seem to be the barrier most people believe it to be.

31. Even a taste of ownership motivates employees.

How about employees all the way down the line and through the corporation? How do we align them to the goals and strategies of the enterprise? Obviously for the appropriate individuals, a bonus program aligned to the department's goals is appropriate. But how about awarding stock options for all employees?

I discovered the power of ownership early in my management career, establishing an employee stock ownership plan (ESOP), once popular as incentive compensation as well as a tax write-off for corporations and even a way to slowly transfer ownership of a company from the founders to the employees. These plans are not as popular today because of their complexity and difficulty to manage, lost in favor of simple stock option plans.

Each month, at the monthly company lunch for all, I'd greet everyone with "Hello shareholders", and proceed to show the assembled throng slides of high level financial statements, pointing out progress against plan. That form of open book management surprises many, but if the employees are stakeholders with a taste of equity, why not underscore the value of that equity by treating them as cohorts? Yes, sometimes the news is not good. They should know this, and from you not from the rumor mill. Your fear that the confidential information may get out to the industry competitors should be tempered by the fact that you are not giving out the secret sauce, just the results of the past period's performance.   All public companies including your public competitors must do this in greater detail each quarter, and it rarely damages their ability to sell into the marketplace. Would bad news drive your best employees out the door? Perhaps. But it is my experience with many companies that empowered employees, treated with respect and shared knowledge, will go far beyond expectation in remaining loyal to their associates and their employer.

And think of the time saved around the virtual water cooler if there are far fewer rumors to pass among your employees.

32. Review regularly. Act upon results.

Allowing small problems to escalate into big ones is simple. Just ignore the signs for long enough and the job is done. It takes far more energy to review regularly the key performance indicators you've established for each individual and yourself. But a small excursion caught early and corrected saves massive corrective resources later.

Take for example the manufacturing company with a small quality problem in one component, resulting in a test failure rate above the norm. You can just reject the components, especially if coming from an outside supplier, or you can get to the root of the problem by examining the cause and reengineering the process or product quickly, saving you and perhaps your supplier time and cost. Such a culture of quality engineering has an additional benefit in creating a higher bar for all to see, making the public statement that quality is a top priority.

The same careful management applies to virtually every person and process in the organization. If there are ways to measure successful output or execution, find them and use them regularly. If one person or department is not pulling its weight, others notice and if no action is taken, often others are discouraged because of the lack of management interest and control. The variant of "one bad apple" holds true in corporate cultures to a degree entrepreneurial managers and young CEOs rarely credit – until a late correction is made and a collective sigh of relief can be heard company-wide.

33. Virtual startups are no stigma.

Rent your first office with caution.

Recently, I became involved with a Southeast Asian company looking to expand into the United States. During the discussions with the CEO about hiring North American managers, he made it clear that he wanted us to find a first class office facility from which to start the search process, and proceeded to name cities that attracted him. Even after discouraging him from this backwards method of infrastructure-building, he kept bringing up the subject in subsequent months as new senior managers and sales people were hired, each starting with an orientation week at the Asian headquarters then returning to work from home. With audio and video conferencing and all the tools for communication and collaboration available today, each of these four new employees felt empowered, connected and enthused to work from home for the first time. The Asian CEO was still talking about finding an office when the natural progression of growth made it obvious that two of the four needed to be replaced. These two worked from homes in widely scattered cities. Had the office been located to accommodate either one, the company would have had to find replacements in the same geographical area as the office. Without that restriction, outstanding replacements were located based upon skill and experience, not location.

Very early stage businesses, start-ups, actually benefit from the establishment of a virtual environment. The flexibility in hiring decisions, reduced fixed costs, forced highly specific communications and better definition of job responsibilities that most often result from need, almost always give a virtual startup the edge financially and flexibly.

So can a startup exist for a reasonably long time as a virtual company? A decade ago there was a stigma that prevented many CEO's from thinking it possible. Today, virtual offices are accepted at all levels of many organizations of all sizes.

34. Well-managed employees work well from home.

Do home-based employees work with the same dedication and productivity as those in office cubicles next to each other? That depends upon the management as much as the employee. I have a friend who is a CEO of a recruiting firm who "virtualized" her company after a decade of maintaining a fixed office location. She organizes morning conference calls, has each employee tweet the others in their department when starting work and ending the day, creates the feel of closeness with employee contests, and rewards her best sales people by assigning them the best leads, creating an environment where the best excel and those unable to cut it in a virtual environment fall out on their own accord for lack of revenue. But most important, the unpredicted benefit of having very low infrastructure overhead may be the one most important element in saving the company during the strongest and longest downturn in recruiting industry memory because of the recent recession. Much larger recruiting companies are in trouble, with high fixed costs for facilities that cannot be shed quickly. This CEO's decision to try to retain an excellent, motivated staff in a virtual environment is paying off in every way. The employees are more satisfied, actually work more hours in a day even if spread over a longer period, and uniformly claim a better lifestyle as a result of the move.

But as you see from the story above, it does take more creative management to make this work. It is a management skill that was not taught nor learned until recent times. A creative CEO will find ways to motivate and compensate for the lone nature of working alone, but using social networking tools to make office workers and home workers feel and behave as a unit. After all, with this generation of texting, tweeting, IM-based workforce, you'll find as much of this kind of communication from adjacent cubicles as from distant home offices.

Let's pause for a word about dress code and formal accountability for the home office worker. Employees working at home must dress for work, even if casual, and find a schedule for the start of each work day that is to be counted upon by fellow workers. It won't be long before home workers will routinely greet each other via video conference from the home desk. Although possible today and used by some, it is not a requirement of most employers with home-based workers. Someone who "comes to work each day" even if to the computer in a separate part of an apartment, is putting on the business hat in a much more formal way that one who drifts to a computer in the room beside a blaring TV, dressed in pajamas and arriving whenever convenient.

How about the employee unable to self-motivate in a home environment? With the proper measurements of productivity, it will soon become quite obvious to both the employee and manager that such an opportunity is not right for that person.

Ask any CEO who has tried letting employees work from home, whether for a day a week or as a rule with occasional office visits. You'll find stories of emails time stamped well into the night, work performed at unusual hours and productivity increases. You'll also hear a bit of pride in the telling. A CEO that encourages this once-risky venture and is rewarded with increased performance, is a person fulfilled and willing to tell anyone who'll listen.

Now we move to the dark side with stage six as we examine how good CEOs hedge against downturns and reduce risks while focusing upon growth opportunities.

Chapter Six. HEDGING AGAINST DOWNTURNS

The importance of this stage in a business's development is particularly obvious after the recession experiences of most CEO's. When times are good, many of us tend to forget the downside risks and aggressively move to grow with little resources in reserve. Ask the members of the generation that lived through the great depression and you'll find near uniformity in their fear that there must be well-planned reserves for contingencies, short and long term. That lesson was not learned by the young tech entrepreneurs who found themselves whipped by the burst of the tech bubble in 2001. For most of the fragile small startups of that period, there was no opportunity to retreat effectively. Money and markets dried up within short months, and unproven business models became risks far too great for investors to maintain. With no proven model and little in the way of reserves, many small tech startups just disappeared, teaching very little to the entrepreneurs who lost everything in the process.

We will assume for this discussion that the business has come far enough to have an indentified, proven market and revenues that greatly reduce the cash burn or have made the company stable through breakeven or beyond performance. Equally, important, we are examining the opportunities for entrepreneurial relatively young businesses, as opposed to large enterprises with large work forces and a long record of predictable performance.

35. Short term leases early on. Move as you grow.

Avoid long-term commitments.

It is statistically true that at least half of the young companies funded by angel or venture investors will not survive three years from funding to demise. The greatest burden of either a growing company or one needing to retract and reduce expenses is the office lease. Although payroll is almost always the greatest cost, companies have flexibility as to how to handle both rapid growth and rapid decline in the personnel arena.

The most difficult thing to deal with in either rapid growth or retrenchment is the office lease. A five year lease may be cheaper than a three year lease, and may provide for more free rent and tenant improvements. Those benefits pale in comparison to the high cost in retaining or buying out a longer term lease.

From personal experience with many companies in my portfolio and from many board experiences over the years, young companies are unpredictably unstable in their facilities requirements. Flexibility is worth a few percentage points of fixed cost when companies are in high growth mode or are at early stages of proof of market.

It is a hassle to move, requiring time and planning. It is much worse to worry over paying for two leases each month and tying up two large deposits. Then there is the dread of "The tyranny of the new office" to worry about. But that is a story for the next insight...

36. Pay for frequent moves over risky long leases.

One of the most obvious observations I make with growing company CEO's is that planning for a new office is done with an optimistic view of the future, incorporating planned space that compromises only slightly the measured needs for the next three or more years as outlined in the financial forecast.

The result, signing a lease for space enough to handle the growth called for in the plan, is a predictable group behavior I've come to label *"The tyranny of the new office."* The company plans a move to a new facility with plenty of space that is probably built out but not planned for use until the company grows to the next stage of need. Employees move into their new cubicles and offices, spread out far more than in the previous facility. The excitement and noise of working in too-close proximity to cohorts suddenly becomes an unexpected near silence, as everyone notices that they do not have to raise their voices any more to be heard above the din of noise.

The exciting sounds of an office filled to capacity functioning in a growth environment are exhilarating to most that have experienced it. The distractions are dealt with using iPods and earphones, concentration and tolerance; but they are dealt with by all. The change to a near silent environment is so startling that, many times, employees express a bit of resentment or even depression, masked by the common statement that "it is so much easier to get work done without the noise." It is the excitement of activity that generates more and better output for most, not the isolation of silence.

But back to "the tyranny of the new office." Two predictable outcomes almost always follow a move into an office much larger than today's needs. First, you'll find subtle moves by employees into the unused, reserved space. After all, it is there and unneeded for now. Why not make use of the space until needed? And second, management sees the open space and often finds it easier to justify acceleration of one or more new hires since the facility is available and infrastructure complete.

Unconsciously longing for a bit more of the excitement from the noise of the previous office, managers often make subtle unrecognized moves to fill the void with new hires earlier than plan. That's why the label, "tyranny" even if the word seems out of context.

If and when asked, I always recommend more frequent moves as opposed to longer term leases. It seems from experience that both the company and the employees gain from such staggered moves.

It is time to examine the CEO's relationships with contemporaries, coaches, good board members and great resources in the community and industry.

Chapter Seven. SURROUNDING YOURSELF WITH TALENT

A great CEO is not afraid to listen to and take advice from experienced players in business and the industry. With the ease of today's communication in its many frictionless forms over the Internet, I find myself giving and getting advice about specific problems without the usual social time spent in personal communication. You've got to know and be comfortable with the person on the opposite end of the keyboard or Skype video, but it works.

In fact, great CEO's invite help and welcome criticism and guidance. In this stage of a business's development, we'll explore the insights relating to finding, nurturing, compensating and acting upon advice from coaches, board members and advisors.

37. An experienced coach has seen your movie before.

Business coaches come in all sizes and shapes. You'll have a relative willing to devote time, a school friend with business experience, professionals who charge for the service, investors with a reason to promote your success and more.

But by far the best coaches are those that have lived through the process you're going through and built successful enterprises in your same industry. Especially if they have sold their companies and live comfortably upon the proceeds, these people are often the most willing to help and the most patient through the process.

One great source for coaches is among fellow members of a CEO roundtable organization, Young Presidents Organization or similar association where you are comfortable with the coach candidate and know something about his or her style. Another is through industry associations or civic groups such as Rotary or Lions Club. Some larger communities have organizations of corporate directors, composed of a combination of service providers and professional corporate directors.

If you take smart money from a good angel or venture organization, the lead investor usually becomes your board member and has a vested interest in your success. If you are lucky enough to create competition among investors for your company, you can select the investor or group with an individual who has experience in your niche and identifies with your vision.

How do you pay a coach? If the coach is also a significantly large investor such as a VC fund, the board member-coach will offer a limited amount of time outside of board work at no extra cost, all for the good of the investment. Professional advisors, consultants, are typically paid by the half day or full day, charging anywhere from $400 per half day at the low end up to $3,000 or more at the high end for a full day of work. Some charge by the hour, making themselves available much as an attorney, keeping track of hours spent on phone calls and emails with you. And some will willingly work for stock options, an amount to be negotiated based upon time spent and stage of corporate development. Years ago, I co-wrote my first book, profiling just such a person, trading his time and experience in exchange for equity - and managing to become wealthy in the process by picking and aiding great young companies that grew large and were ultimately sold at a tremendous profit. We had no term for such work in those days, and created the phrase "resource capitalist" to describe the person and process. He brought resources to the table from personal experience to a great contact base, and was able to help speed the time to market while introducing the company to great potential buyers at the right time in the process. His average percentage of a company was 5% in return for spending a day a week as I recall.

Jokingly, I used to tell people that I worked for food, with so many free lunches being offered from all sides. But alas, there is no free lunch. And over the years I have vastly curtailed the practice. However, there surely are experienced executives out there who'll work for a meal. It is worth asking.

There must be many more creative ways to pay a coach, especially for early stage businesses. The one warning: avoid those looking to become partners, asking for larger portions of equity than, say, 5% when they contribute no cash to the enterprise. There may be times when such a person can truly be a founding partner in a young business and devote enough time and resources to warrant more, but this is taking on a partner in every sense of the word, and should be done carefully and only after spending time with a number of the person's references and becoming comfortable with the person, ready for the long run.

38. Surround yourself with great, sharing advisors.

This insight addresses the establishment and maintenance of an advisory board, a formal group with no legal responsibilities, but one able to be called upon to act as business, industry and scientific advisors to the CEO. Usually, such an advisory board is formed carefully by the CEO to fill in the critical areas of need not evidenced in the board of directors or within the company itself. University professors, industry gurus, lawyers familiar with patent law and former executives of competitor companies are typical recruits to an advisory board. Sometimes, celebrities will agree to sit on an advisory board as a gift to the CEO, providing a bit of glamour for the company at small expense.

There is no limit to the number of individuals for such a board, but there is a practical limit to the amount of cash and / or stock to be allocated to these outside advisors. The rule of thumb for an advisory board member is to expect a full day each year on site, typically in a strategic planning meeting with numerous members of the staff, and a number of phone calls from senior members of management during the year. Included in the "package" is the expectation that the advisor's name will be freely used in the company's marketing, a bio listed on the website, and occasional calls will come as references to the advisor from potential investors and others looking for deeper insight into the secret sauce of the company or state of the industry than can be provided by many on the inside. For this, an advisory board member for a small to medium sized company should expect to receive options equal to ¼% of the fully diluted stock of the company, vesting over two years, and subsequent grants of the same size if renewed in subsequent two year intervals. Alternatively, some companies pay an advisor a fee of $1,000 per meeting day and optionally much smaller stock grants, if any. Additional commitments of time by an advisory board member should be compensated as would any consultant, at half and full day rates agreed upon in advance between the CEO and the advisor. There is no rule as to uniformity of pay, as some advisors may be willing to serve at no cost while others are industry consultants used to receiving fair payment for services rendered.

I sit on a board of a company with potentially valuable patents that it is exploiting aggressively. The board has hired an attorney firm to pursue protection of these patents in the courts, but the members of the board felt that it would be wise to add a member to the advisory board who is also a patent attorney to watch over the process and advise the board at its meetings of issues that may not have been covered by the paid attorney or by other member of the board itself. In this case, payment for the attorney advisory board member was agreed to in the form of common stock options more generous than the average advisory board grant, as the attorney was invited to sit in on all meetings of the corporate board and agreed to do so. There are many variants of the rule for payment, and many reasons why advisors may be willing to serve. In this instance, the attorney realizes that the potential value of the stock options in the event of major wins in patent litigation would far outweigh any fees which he might have charged.

Advisors fill blind spots in the corporate knowledge base and guide the CEO in areas that the CEO feels are personal weaknesses. There is usually a formal agreement between the company and the advisor, carefully calling out the time expectation, the forms and amounts of payment, and the indemnifications from liability granted by the company to the advisor in return for confidentiality and non-disclosure of company trade secrets by the advisor.

A particularly strong advisor, especially if well known, may be named chairman of the advisory board, often just a honorary title, since the CEO is usually tasked with the planning of the full day meeting of advisors annually, setting the agenda to match the needs of the member of the corporate board and senior management.

39. Outside directors are a price of investment.

Once a company founder has tapped the funds available from his or her resources and from friends and family, if the company needs more cash for growth, the most obvious next step is to look for money from angel investors and venture capitalists, typically in the $300,000 TO $3,000,000 range. This money comes with restrictions a founder may not expect, including restrictions upon the sale of founder stock, clauses that require the investor be allowed to sell an equal proportion of stock upon any other person's sale of stock, anti-dilution provisions that protect the investor from a subsequent offer of stock at a lower price, and much more. Almost always, professional investors, including angel groups and venture capitalists, also require at least one seat on the corporate board. The investor organization is granted the seat as long as the investment remains, and the documents often name the first representative assigned by the investor group to the position.

In subsequent insights, we will explore the legal and ethical responsibilities of board members. But the intent of these "forced" placements of a representative on the board is obviously to watch over the company's use of invested funds and to help grow the company in value. The combination of restrictive covenants in the investor documents and the new dynamic of board members with an agenda make for a change in the culture of the corporation, certainly one for the CEO.

However, outside professional investor board members can be a very good asset to the corporation with the skills, experience and broad relationships many bring to the boardroom table.

40. Great relationships are among your most valuable assets.

As you follow these insights from ignition to liquidity event, you'll detect a continuing theme, emphasizing the need for deep and wide relationships that the CEO and senior staff can call upon for advice and guidance. This is the time to elevate those insights to the level of highest value for the corporation, one that cannot be listed on a balance sheet nor included in an appraisal of corporate worth. And yet, such relationships properly used and never overused, can quickly and precisely help a CEO cut through delays in government agencies, speed the process of product planning and ultimate release, aid in positioning in the market and help the CEO avoid a myriad of mistakes that could prove costly in time and money.

Often, I am asked by young CEO's how much time should be devoted to various types of tasks by a good CEO in a small, growing enterprise.   Of course the response depends upon lots of variables, including whether the company is in a fund-raising mode (in which case the CEO may be spending up to 80% of his or her time on this alone). I am chairman of a CEO roundtable organization with multiple CEO roundtables of about twelve members each, meeting monthly. Each CEO is asked to make a deep presentation once a year in which he or she starts with personal and business goals for the coming year followed by concerns as to how to reach these goals. Much of the rest of the presentation is devoted to explaining to the group the causes for the concerns and offering information for the group to use in the feedback session to help the CEO seek solutions and to provide resources to the CEO for that purpose. The format also calls for the CEO to examine his calendar over a period of time and report classes of activities by percentage of total time spent, so that the group may add comments about use of CEO time to the critique. It is from over a thousand of these CEO presentations over the years that I attempt to make these generalities.

A good CEO spends at least 30% of his or her time dealing with customers, including meeting directly with customers and being involved in closing the largest deals, maintaining CEO relationships, and "sniffing" the attitudes of customers toward the company as well as exploring the needs of the customer that might be satisfied by new product development. 15% typically is spent on direct management issues such as supervision of next level subordinates. 15% might be spent networking with those in the CEO's relationship circle, including the roundtable organizations. 10% is typically spent networking with board members, usually with frequent phone calls, and preparing for board meetings. 10% is typical in exploring strategic concepts, reading about new developments in the industry and just spending quiet time contemplating opportunities. There are many other classes a typical CEO will list, some concentrating upon time spent in meetings of all kinds, lumped together as if all meetings are of some equal value. The group often pays close attention when this happens, since it is a sign that the CEO considers meetings of all kinds a drain upon available time, and few meetings of special importance. Whatever, the spread of percentages to make 100% of a CEO's time, the CEO is asked to estimate the average number of hours spent each week at or on work. Most respond with between 60 and 80 hours a week, emphasizing what you already know, that CEO's are not often 40 hour workers. But then again, in this new world of always-on communications, who is?

41. Associate with competitors. Share carefully.

Many of us belong to industry associations and find ourselves at conferences and trade shows with time to spend with competitors. Some of these are old friends; some even former associates. It is natural to want to associate with these people for many reasons, certainly socially. Most CEO's want to obtain information about their competitors in the most subtle and non-obvious ways. And of course, most are willing to trade information to get information.

In my former industry, I became an informal centralized source for knowledge about the revenues of each of the many competitors, with a special skill for asking just the right questions to obtain the information. How many employees does the firm have today? Are you profitable yet? Can you guess what percentage your revenue comes from recurring sources such as maintenance revenues? In return for the answers to these several questions, I was usually able to guess a company's gross revenues within a few percent and would state my guess to the CEO. His reaction would guide me to increase or decrease my estimate appropriately. He'd be a bit amazed with the quick fancy math work, and I would have yet another piece of the puzzle helping me to gauge the total size of the industry in annual revenues and the growth and size of competitors. All of this was immensely helpful in strategic planning and marketing, even though to this day I do not think those CEOs were aware of the value of the information so easily given. And none of this is especially considered a trade secret, violating the unspoken covenant between competitor CEOs that there is a limit to such exchanges.

On the other hand, often a sales person or marketing manager would show up at my door with a complete package of a competitor's materials, including price lists, a proposal with discount percentages clearly shown and a list of feature functionality meant to reinforce the proposal. The source of this information was typically the purchasing decision-maker for a friendly customer or candidate customer. The question is one of ethics, since the competitor certainly did not volunteer any of the information, which would have been the competitor employee's violation of confidentiality and cause for being fired. What does a CEO do with this wonderful, rich information dropped at his door at no cost or obligation? Few would destroy it and ask all to forget that it was ever in their hands. Most would absorb the information and then admonish those who had seen it to not repeat to anyone that it was in their hands. If you've been in business for long enough, you've seen your share of this gray market information. My only advice is to use it carefully, never ever publicly, and certainly never reproduce it, let alone disseminate it internally.

As to sharing information to get information, CEO's and executives are bound by a duty to their corporations not to share trade secrets with anyone who has not signed a confidentiality agreement, including consultants to the company. For CEOs on the corporate board, it is a large part of the "duty of care", a legal requirement of board members to protect the assets of the corporation first and foremost, one of those assets being the trade secrets of the corporation.

42. The value of legal advice isn't measured by a law degree.

Over the years in business and as a member of over forty boards over the years, I have received good advice from corporate attorneys and on occasion bad advice as well. There is a line that should be drawn in a relationship between corporate attorney and CEO or board. Attorneys are paid to protect the corporation, not to give business advice. Some are experienced enough to provide great business advice. But the law degree they earned does not assure that, even though most CEO's respect the advice they receive from their attorney highly enough not to doubt the conclusions or the experience behind the conclusions offered. And since attorneys are paid to protect, often they will give a litany of warnings about what could go wrong when accepting a contract clause they have been trained to challenge. There comes a time when a CEO must decide to reject what may seem like important good advice from the attorney and chance acceptance of terms within a contract that may cause risk, but controllable risk or risk that is so remote as to be worth the acceptance of the business represented by the contract at hand.

I was chairman of a company that had been offered an investment by a Fortune 500 company making a strategic investment in our business, which was capable of driving new demand to the large company though a series of new web services creating a greater need for the large company's products. The business terms had been agreed to between the business development officer of the investing company and our board, as both companies turned the details over to their respective attorneys for documentation. The attorney for the investor was a member of a large, respected law firm in Silicon Valley, and certainly was full of himself as sole legal protector of the rights of his very significant investor. As drafts of the otherwise standard investment agreements passed from him to our attorney and our management, we immediately spotted a significant number of terms we not only had not agreed to but were contrary to the spirit of the investment. The attorney held fast at every challenge, stating that "these terms are standard for our client and cannot be changed." We appealed to the business development executive, who deferred to the attorney restating that the terms were unchangeable as far as the big company was concerned. After conferring between our attorney and board, we walked away from what would have been a fine strategic partnership, killed by an attorney who probably understood the client requirements but was unwilling to offer flexible solutions to problem areas. That attorney had made what we considered business decisions on behalf of his client. By the way, we immediately found a willing replacement that had an attorney not quite so full of himself and quickly concluded a similar deal to the acceptance of all. And to this day, I caution my CEO's not to deal with that Fortune 500 firm because of the experience we had with its attorney. You never know how much far reaching an action can be, given the speed and extent of communication between CEO's today.

43.   Accountants "plan-alyze". Bookkeepers count beans.

This is a distinction we need to repeat on occasion, especially for new CEO's looking to pay a low wage for advanced financial analysis, whether with an independent contractor or an employee. Accountants are trained, certified and usually quite experienced in financial analysis, both creating and reviewing data. Bookkeepers are often trained on the job although sometimes more formally, and handle the physical work of accounting for the transactions. To expect a bookkeeper to provide analytical planning is to ask for something they often cannot provide, except in a cursory way.

Why the discussion? Many early stage CEO's believe they can delegate design and creation of metrics, flash reports, analytical reports and more from their bookkeepers. And at some early stages, a bookkeeper is capable of preparing such information. It does not take long for a growing business and a knowledgeable CEO to quickly outgrow the lack of depth and sophistication such reporting usually offers, looking instead for deeper analytical tools.

On the other hand, many early stage CEO's are not trained and ready for such tools even if available. The lesson here is twofold. There is a benefit to using a good accountant to help devise critical reports for a corporation; and CEO's must quickly become financially savvy in the analysis of financial statements and metrics that measure the health of a business. To fail to have this skill is to reduce the corporation's capability to discover problems early and take advantage of growth opportunities.

44. Good tax planning is both legal and smart.

When do you cross the line between honesty and dishonesty in tax planning? Is it ethical to allocate income between periods to take advance of tax breaks? Can expenses be put off until the next period to increase income, or accelerated into this period by prepayment to decrease net income? Where do you draw the line, assuming no intent to defraud?

First, corporations are usually on an accrual accounting basis, meaning that income and expenses are accounted for as earned, not when the cash is received. (You, on the other hand, account for your individual income on a cash-accounting bases, counting the cash not the date of your earning or accrued expense. The difference: If you earn pay due December 31st and it is paid January second, you pay income tax on those earnings in the following year. But the corporation that pays you accrues the expense and takes the deduction in the year in which the income was earned or expense actually incurred.)

It is perfectly legal to hold delivery of goods until after the start of the next period and take the income next year rather than this. It is a bit murky if you accelerate payment for incomplete services or even for products not yet received into this year to take the deduction from income early. In either an IRS audit or an accounting review or audit, the accelerated costs and payments will show as an accrual – a balance sheet item – that does not change income, just cash and an asset. In other words, for the usual accrual-based business, there are fewer ways to affect the outcome than for a cash-accounting individual. There are lots of caveats here and certainly if the issue is critical to you, an accountant (rarely a bookkeeper) should guide you to the action that is both legal and strategic.

45. Consultants are only as good as the as the advice you take.

At one time or another, most all businesses use consultants to fill the gaps in knowledge or to provide guidance for management. Consultants are good in that you can sample their work with short projects, change to other consultants quickly, and stop using them when a project is completed.

I have a partner in a consulting practice that specializes in the travel industry. Several years ago, we were hired by one of the largest companies in the industry (yet another Fortune 500) to perform a top-to-bottom audit of their processes across 27 facilities, and recommend measures to increase efficiency, increase income and of course, decrease costs while also increasing the quality of service. We were quite confident that our services would yield great, measurable results. The work continued for about eight weeks between the two of us as we visited the 27 locations and worked with employees in departments across all disciplines within each location and at central offices that performed services for all locations.

Finally, at the end of the project, we had identified nineteen specific issues, each of which would, if implemented, accomplish one or more of the goals outlined at the start of the project. The sum of the savings and increases in revenue were worth multi-millions annually, well worth the implementation of most or all of the recommendations.

On the final day of our assignment, I was responsible for the "reporting out" to the assembled twenty or so executives in the large conference room of this major corporation. I started my presentation, which had been carefully documented in handouts and PowerPoint, with this story...

"I want you to all imagine that it is tomorrow morning, looking back upon today's reporting of these past months of work by your consultants. Imagine that today I build for you a beautiful sand castle exactly at the water line of the ocean nearby. Tomorrow, we both will visit that beach and look at the water line, and find not a beautiful castle, but just smooth sand, just as it had been the day before building our beautiful sand castle. In other words, I would not be surprised if you accept our report today with enthusiasm, but then in the overwhelming rush of daily business, fail to implement few if any of these recommendations that you so enthusiastically received."

The story is true and the results were as I predicted. A few of the recommendations were implemented over time, one with great effect and even a national advertising campaign behind it (that you surely saw on TV). But most were just ignored. I imagine that our report sits today on someone's shelf, filed with others from past and from following months and years.

Unfortunately, it is human nature to enthusiastically ignore to act upon recommendations of third party consultants. There are many, many exceptions, but far more instances of this in the business world. Not all consultants give advice worth taking, of course. But when they do so, it is only as good as that which you implement.

46. Boards of directors protect the corporation first.

All other board functions are secondary.

Even venture capitalists who sit on boards where they have significant investments often forget this point. They write into their investment documents that they will occupy a seat on the board for as long as they are invested in the company, thinking of this as a protection for their investment and tool for them to influence growth.

Actually, there are two legal duties of board members. They are: *the duty of care*, and the *duty of loyalty*. Everything else is a self-imposed duty or responsibility. The duty of care is to care for the corporation asset itself, not the shareholders whom they represent. Each corporation when chartered becomes a live person in the eyes of the law, independent and subject to the care of its board of directors. Shareholders such as the investors are granted few rights by law. They can elect directors for their class of stock, approve mergers and acquisitions; approve increases or changes to the capital structure of the company and other more minor actions. It is the board, made up of individual members, that is responsible for the care and maintenance of the corporate person. Sometimes, there will be a conflict of interest between the people representing the various shareholder classes on a board. This happens often when one class would be quite satisfied with the outcome of a sale of the corporation because it has lower expectations of exit value and a lower cost of shares, while another later investor class would see little relative gain in a sale and veto's the proposed transaction. The duty of care is a legal responsibility of each board member and cannot be shed because the member was elected to protect a particular class of shareholder.

Second is the duty of loyalty – loyalty to the corporate person, not to the shareholders who elected the board member. Once again, there is a need to educate board members that in conflict of interest cases, the corporation comes first. Some investor board members are also member of boards for companies that may overlap in markets or even compete directly, although rare. Either way, I have seen many instances over the years of my board service with VC's on the board, which the VC's have had information about other firms that would be classified as confidential - that they offered at least piecemeal in a board meeting of another company where they serve. There are issues that stress the loyalty of board members such as placement of employees or recruiting of executives from firms where the VC or board member has inside knowledge. These are rare, but each stresses the duty of loyalty to the corporation on whose board they sit.

Should board members therefore withdraw and not participate in corporate planning, coaching the CEO and other issues not related to the duty of care or duty of loyalty? Of course they should not. A board, in exercising its duty of care, must do everything it can as an entity and each member as an individual to become acquainted with the issues, problems, opportunities and threats that overhang the corporation. In fact, there is a legal concept (not a duty) of "reasonable care" that board members must meet in order to be protected by the insurance carried by a company for directors and officers. Reasonable care means that members deliberate issues in depth, attract expert advice when appropriate, attend meetings regularly, stay current on corporate issues and hold regular sessions of the outside directors without management present. None of these requirements are by law, but the sum of these add to a powerful statement of commitment by board members and therefore a protection under the law when a group of shareholders sue boards or members for irresponsible actions. Most every court will side with the members of the board under the rule of reasonable care when these behaviors are in evidence.

47. The need for a board grows with complexity.

Start-ups with one founder rarely have or need a board of directors. In fact, such a board would seem out of place in a one person company. As soon as any outside money is ingested into the corporation, others have a vested and legal interest in the behavior of officers entrusted with the best use of funds. Money from friends and family usually is offered in a casual manner with much less restriction than professional investors, so that a formal board is a logical step but not often created upon this event. Then along comes either money or contracts from strategic or financial investors or partners. The operations of the corporation become more complex. Ownership is spread among several classes of investors. The number of employees grows. Bank loans with restrictive covenants are taken on. These events, one or all, usually are triggers for the founders to seek to create a board for oversight and guidance.

Once created, it is logical to follow the standard practice in the creation of two standing committees composed of outside board members (not employees or executives) – the compensation committee and the audit committee. Compensation's charter is to approve stock option grants for any employee, not matter how small the grant, and all salary and benefits for at least the CEO if not the next level down, to avoid conflict of interest with the CEO. All actions of the committee are in the form of recommendations to the full board for vote, and are not binding until that event.

Second, the audit committee is responsible for hiring an outside auditor as appropriate, reviewing the accounting practices of the corporation and making sure that laws are followed relating to recognition of revenues and expenses. Good audit committees also review the corporation's insurance portfolio, risk protection policies such as email and computer use, disaster response and recovery policies and any other area where the corporation's very life could be at risk from inattention.

Let me tell you the story of a company on whose board I sat for several years. The CEO insisted that between husband and wife, over half the stock always be in their hands, refusing new offerings or any other form of dilution, and controlling the majority of board seats in the process. After replacing two board members with two other friends who were a bit less independent, during that first meeting with all present including the two new board members, I suggested that the corporation then form the two committees – audit and compensation. "Never!" was the single word as I recall the CEO's immediate outburst. I made a motion to bring it to a vote. The corporate attorney was present, recommending this as a relatively safe move for the CEO. I called the question after a drifting discussion. You can guess that the three friends voted down the measure, perhaps as a sign of unison, since this was the first vote by the two new members. It was the final nail for me. I engineered the extraction of the outside investors, even at a near total loss. At least the investors could then take the loss against ordinary income under rule 1244 of the IRS code, worth something to each, rather than being locked into what was a slowly failing lifestyle business with no effective oversight.

48. Fight for balance on your board.

In my last insight, I described the CEO who stacked the board with two friends, making a majority for control purposes and relegating the investor representatives to insignificance. There were no outside board members with industry experience, no members the CEO trusted with governance backgrounds, no scientists to evaluate the technology that is the core asset of the corporation.

If the CEO does not do so, outside board members must fight for balance on a board. If for no other reason, this protects the members of the board from making decisions without rising to the standard of careful deliberation under the "reasonable care" test.

Some boards find themselves debating whether there should be an expansion from five to seven, from seven to nine or more in order to allow for such a mixture of protective seats created by the investment documents and balance with outside board members. Sometimes, as in one board where I sit today, there are so many classes of investors, each with one or more seats, that a seven person board is not enough. I am not for large boards. There are social studies that reinforce the notion that a group of six or seven is far more likely to arrive at reasoned decisions effectively than larger groups. Look at the example of most non-profit boards, where the number of members often exceeds thirty, requiring the creation of an executive committee to actually get the work done.

49. Board members should be elected annually.

No board member should be grandfathered, guaranteed a board seat forever.

Practically speaking, this is an impossible goal. We have investigated the restrictions imposed by investment documents and the obvious need to keep continuity on the board with the retention of the CEO position at the very least. But it would be the best of forms to require in the bylaws of a corporation that all seats are re-elected annually.

For non-profits, this allows for the creation of a board development committee to find and recruit outstanding new board members and find ways to unseat those who are no longer contributing or even attending board meetings. Such a policy further reinforces the duty of care for the corporation by its board. Unseated board members with longevity and a history of participation can be invited to become "emeriti" members of the board with observation rights but no vote.

Although not required by all corporate bylaws, all companies should hold and document an annual shareholder meeting in which the shareholders are notified at least 20 days in advance and given the right to submit a proxy vote for their choice of officers and for any other issues that will come to a vote, including expansion of the stock option plan to include more available shares.

The bottom line is that good corporate governance calls for a skill set within the board that is not often present, but for protection of the members and the corporation itself, necessary.

50. Good board members are as valuable as good executives.

Perhaps this is the natural conclusion from the several insights previously explored. While the CEO and management offers the vision, strategies and tactics as well as the proposed budget, it is the board that controls with its votes the execution of strategy, the expenditure of cash, the taking on of debt or new equity, the very direction of the company as well as its ultimate health.

The most important person in a corporation usually is and should be the CEO. This person, often the founder in early stage companies and beyond, is the originator and keeper of the vision, leading all others below and the board above as willing believers in the vision advanced. But the board is responsible for providing resources to fulfill that vision, which may include new cash infusion or assumption of new debt.

In extreme situations, it is the board that must step up and replace the CEO, assuming the responsibility for finding and integrating a new leader quickly and efficiently. Sometimes this means having a board member step in for a short time as CEO for continuity. Recently, one of the CEO's in a roundtable had been active and vibrant for years in both his company and the roundtable, died suddenly of a heart attack. His board met in emergency session and managed a smooth transition to a new leader within a month, during the most traumatic of times for all employees and the board itself. For non-profit boards, the two most important duties under the duty of loyalty and care are the oversight and eventual replacement of the CEO, and maintenance of the entity over its infinitely long lifetime. I have been member and even chair of presidential search committees, and can attest that board members (and other designated stakeholders) spend hundreds of hours in the recruiting process, all without pay.

It is because the continuity provided by the board is the one thing shareholders must count on above all else to protect investment, that the board rises in importance to at least equal stature as the executive cohort.

51. To your directors: *Noses in, fingers out.*

I first heard this in a governance seminar for a non-profit higher educational board upon which I sit, years ago. It made an impact and stuck with me through the years. I have repeated it often to boards deliberating action and to individual board members seeking to get their hands dirty inside the corporation by giving advice and helping at levels beneath the CEO.

The problem cannot be overstated. Once a board member reaches beyond the CEO into the corporation, especially without the approval of the CEO, incurable damage has been done to the CEO's ability to govern. Even if not the intent, there is an instant change in dynamic once this line has been crossed.

There is even a gray area that illustrates this effectively. As chairman of a company in an industry where I have extensive experience, I elected to attend a regular meeting of the management team with its middle managers on a Monday morning, a practice I had not done in the past. The meeting was tame to say the least. The CEO spoke, shared metrics, spoke of issues to be addressed during the coming week, and did a fine job of pointing the assembled troops in the right direction. I could not have been more pleased. After returning to my office, I received a call from the CEO. 'Would I please (oh, don't take this wrong, Dave) not attend these meetings anymore?' What I took for unusual silence was a complete disruption of the normal give and take of the management group because of my presence. The chairmanship carries unstated power even if not overtly demonstrated, since the CEO reports to and is accountable to the board, and of course its chair. I learned from this that there are times when members of the board are appropriately brought into an operating group, and certainly times when the board should hear from vice presidents presenting their issues in a board meeting. But the position of CEO is absolutely to be reinforced at all costs, never to be undermined by any member or by the board as an entity.

Therefore, it is appropriate to ask the tough questions, request help in understanding issues, seek permission from the CEO to interview others. But a board member should never react to statements heard by issuing directions or hints of board action in return. It is appropriate to state that the board member understands much more after the briefing and will better be able to address the problem with the board and CEO. It is not appropriate for a board member to promise any action to anyone beneath the level of CEO. Noses in; fingers OUT.

52. Feed your board with constant care and attention.

Plan 10% of your time for board relations.

Most all leaders new to the CEO position underestimate this time requirement. It is good for the company when the CEO shares concerns, threats and opportunities with the board. The rule of "no surprises" works well for the longevity of a CEO. But there are always surprises. CEO's should communicate with members of the board if not a committee of the whole as soon as possible when threats to the corporation arise.

Sometimes the CEO wants to obtain concurrence from his board for issues of particular importance to him. It is not bad form to lobby individual board members in the form of a briefing of the issue as the CEO sees it, as long as the board is allowed the time to debate the issue, sometimes requesting an "executive session" of just the outside directors.

All of this board management is time consuming. The CEO is also responsible for preparing the board briefing package before regular board meetings, a time-consuming task if done correctly. The package should contain the issues to be discussed with backup materials for the board to understand the issues. Operating statistics in detail and individual departmental issues that do not rise to the level of board discussion should be included only in an appendix for deeper reading, but not discussion. The CEO should discuss the agenda and board package contents with the chairman (if the chair is a different person), since the chair is tasked with setting the agenda and controlling the meeting.

Does this not appear to add to at least 10% of a CEO's time now that you've seen some of the elements of the task?

53. Early stage boards work for stock options not cash.

Give one percent equity to each outside board member vesting over four years of service.

Many early stage CEOs and board members have asked for some guidance regarding pay and time commitments for board members. Here is my best advice, based upon many boards and many years. Pay early stage board members of companies that are not lifestyle businesses one percent of the fully diluted equity in the form of an option that vests over four years of service. The option price should be set by appraisal under IRS rule 409a, and certainly should be low enough to recognize that common stock options are not worth as much as preferred stock, given the many preferences of the latter. Further, the option should contain a special clause that accelerates vesting to 100% upon a change of control in the corporation, which aligns the board member with the best interests of the corporation itself. Otherwise, you might picture an event in which the sale of a company to be consummated a few months before full vesting could cause a board member to find ways to vote for delays or even against a sale of the company, awaiting full vesting of his or her options.

For lifestyle companies or later stage companies, board members should be paid on a per-meeting basis in cash. Typically this payment amounts to $1,000 per meeting of the board, adjusted upward for public corporations to $3,000 per meeting on average, with special pay for committee chairs and special meetings. These payments recognize that board members are not working for equity but for the equivalent of consulting fees plus the attendant risks of board membership.

Venture investors with investments from their funds are not typically ever offered pay for board service, which is expected as part of the investment. Inside board members, CEO and any other paid employees are not paid for board service in either stock options or cash.

Expenses for travel are often reimbursed by the corporation. VC board members sometimes request this, other times do not. It should not be offered to the VC members unless requested.

The next insight will cover what should be expected of a board member in the way of time allocated to the company.

54. What to expect in board member commitment.

Expect a board member to give a meeting a month, emails and phone calls between. Urgent issues require more of all.

Board members are usually busy people, often running other companies or serving on multiple boards. Early stage boards usually meet once a month for two to four hours, enough to ruin the rest of a day for those who travel even short distances. In addition, most all board members freely receive phone calls and emails from the CEO during the month, all considered part of service.

There are times when board members are called upon to give extra-ordinary time to the corporation, such as interviewing candidates, strategic planning, recovery from cash or other urgent problem issues. Most often these are freely given by board members.

The line is crossed when a CEO asks a member of the board to consult to the company, spending considerable time with other employees regarding issues that might be handled by others than from a board. Depending upon the board member, it is appropriate to offer a consulting fee for this time spent above the call of board duty. Any such informal contracting of service should always be preceded with an agreement between the CEO and board member as to the amount to charge and estimate of time to be spent before further agreement is necessary.

55. D&O insurance is a "cost of respect" for board members.

Whenever there are outside shareholders, and when there is a product in release, there is a chance, no matter how slight, of a lawsuit against members of the board as well as against the corporation itself. Even if such a suit is completely without merit, the cost of defense and the risk of a negative outcome both hang over the company and the director. Directors and Officers insurance is meant to reduce that risk and provide for the legal defense of any such suit at the expense of the insurance company. In that regard, even the lowest amount of D&O insurance available, $1 million, provides for legal defense costs to be covered. The usual cost for such insurance is $4 to $6 thousand a year, with an extra $2 thousand for an additional million of coverage.

More important than the cost is the provision in investment documents from sophisticated investors requiring D&O insurance for the company as of the time of funding.

Over the many years of board service, I have been sued as a director several times, in no case covered under the umbrella of a D&O policy. Although I won each of these rather spurious suits, the cost of defense in some of the cases was not reimbursed, and the time spent in helping the attorney prepare for the defense and in one case through to a several day adjudication event, was not small. As a result, I now insist upon D&O insurance for every board upon which I sit. The backgrounds of these suits make for good stories, but are not appropriate for this telling.

56. Find an outside confidant, a CEO coach.

The CEO position can be a lonely place, especially when the CEO finds himself in a position of not being able to bring an issue directly to the board and not wanting to explore solutions with associates within the company. This sometimes happens when a CEO is unwilling to admit a weakness in an area that is critical, such as analysis of financial statements, or when a CEO is unhappy with the actions of his board or with pay offers by the board's compensation committee that cannot be resolved amicably. Having an experienced coach, usually acting informally and not for any kind of pay, is a safety valve for a CEO that cannot be understated when in times of great stress.

Sometimes that coach is a member of the board willing to listen and make suggestions off the record. And often that is good enough. In my experience, there are times when a CEO needs a completely neutral third party or a roundtable of fellow CEO's to help guide him through a difficult maze.

Develop relationships with fellow CEO's in non-competing businesses for a start. Perhaps even formalize the relationship with regular lunch meetings or meetings in groups of CEO's to discuss personal issues without fear of the discussion leaking outside closed doors.

57. Any advice can be worthless, or worse.

Let me tell you the story of the first investment made by a newly organized formal group of angel investors. It was thrilling for these angels to find a young entrepreneur with an idea for a business that seemed so destined for greatness that the angels invested over $1 million on the condition that the group receive two board seats and one observer seat on the start-up's board. The young, eager entrepreneur agreed immediately and the business was launched, well funded and anticipating great profits.

As the business expanded into a second city and then planned expansion into a third, there was a rift that became evident between these angel board members, played out in front of the CEO. The angels argued about whether the expansion was too quick, requiring additional money, or should be slower and bootstrapped with profits from the first city's success. Finally agreeing upon expansion at speed, the angels raised more money and encouraged the CEO to accelerate the expansion, which the CEO did with enthusiasm. It did not take long for the company to again run out of money, and for the board to split over the next moves (since the first city continued to be profitable).

The angel investors could not raise the next, larger round to finance the shortfall and further expansion, putting the fragile young company at risk for following the advice of its board. In the end, the company had to turn to a wealthy individual investor who took control of the corporation as his price for saving the company. Had the angel board members been able to agree upon a financeable strategy for growth, the company might have been immensely successful. To put an ending to this story, the entrepreneur followed the suggestions of the new investor just as he had the angels, and accelerated quickly into more cities, again running out of cash. The wealthy investor in the meantime, unknown to the CEO or the board, ran into personal trouble with real estate investments, and could not make good on his promise to further fund the company, which found itself unable to meet its obligations and ultimately was shut down, causing a complete loss for all. Bad advice taken by an enthusiastic and compliant young CEO was the root of the cause, compounded by circumstance.

The lesson is for any CEO to filter all advice through the strainer of good reason, taking that which seems reasonable and rejecting that which is wrong for the company or the times. By not putting up any argument and being completely compliant, the CEO ceded control of the company to outsiders who gave bad advice.

58. Make informal advisors part of your team.

Whether you find advisors from family, friends, faculty or fellow managers, great advisors can become an informal resource that rivals that of more formal resources, including board members. You will certainly know when you've found such a treasure, almost always through introduction by others and rarely because you have deliberately approached someone to fill a needed hole. Most of these people will provide time for you out of friendship, rather than seeking reward in the form of stock options or pay for service. Therefore, it is important that you recognize their worth and be most careful not to overuse the gift of their time. "We work for food" is a common mantra for such friends who are willing to provide such informal services.

Are there any rules for the amount of time you might expect before stepping over the line? In my experience both seeking and providing such informal services, personal visits to a company for more than a short time before or after a lunch or dinner are fine. But a scheduled visit for more than a tour and meeting management is asking too much unless offered. These people are not about the pay, and the treasure of their advice is worth the careful use of time in its seeking.

The best use of informal advisors is through phone and emailed short requests for help with a specific issue, one that can be explained easily and rather quickly, and whose resolution may be complex, but with good advice, you can find the way through the problem more quickly and even validate your intuitive answers to a problem.   These informal advisors will appreciate occasional updates in the form of emails just as you would email board members with news of progress.   But such contacts should never be constant or frequent.

Of course, you are free to just drift away from such resources by stopping the calls and emails, most often without being missed and therefore without need to worry over the effect of your inaction. Such advisors, if providing concise and sage responses to questions well asked, are another valuable tool and one without a price tag.

59. Guard the Gold.

Use stock options and warrants to pay for service only rarely.

Earlier, I stated that stock options are the currency of early stage business. This truth is obvious when a start-up has no cash. For this insight, we will assume a business is perhaps well beyond start-up and growing, but that cash is tight, used for growth and for working capital as earned. There are times when services of others are available for stock instead of - or in addition to cash.   Such service providers as web designers, public relations firms, even venture banks granting loans, often offer higher value services for a lesser amount of cash and some amount of stock options or warrants (written promises to sell stock at a set price for a future period in time).

When assessing the relative merit of using attractive non-cash forms of compensation for outside services, first be aware of the true value of your stock. Because the valuation is now a requirement under Rule 409sa of the Internal Revenue Code, most companies with stock option plans today have fairly valued common stock with known prices per share. Second, when making such a decision, assess the speed of growth and risks associated with that growth, as both would affect the value of the common stock. If an imminent fund-raising effort will be undertaken and the corporate growth is slow, it is logical to fear that the next round will be dilutive and perhaps at a lower valuation than the current value per share. But if the growth is strong enough to anticipate increasing stock valuation over time, then the grants of stock instead of cash for services may in the end prove to be quite expensive to the existing shareholders by involuntarily diluting their holdings. It is the same logic larger corporations use when deciding whether to use cash or stock to make an acquisition. If the stock is highly priced, corporations may be quite willing to use their shares as currency for acquisitions. Such an analysis is in the service of all shareholders.

And remember, any grant of shares or options must be approved by the corporate board before issuance, since it changes the capital structure of the corporation, even if the option pool has been previously approved by the board.

We have explored issues related to corporate governance and resources for the top levels of management. It is time to look into the protection of the business enterprise as it grows and acquires or creates wealth and value.

Chapter Eight. PROTECTING THE BUSINESS

There are many stories of good businesses large and small felled by failure to insure against calamities of many unforeseen types. In this phase of our analysis into the stages of a company's life cycle, we investigate the protection of the corporate asset, using commercial tools and insights that cost nothing more than knowledge, with the board and management watching for signs of impending problems both external and internal.

60. Insurance is always too expensive until needed.

This insight seems obvious to most anyone. But it is a fact that business insurance is one of the more poorly managed mitigations of risk in small and some medium sized corporations, often because of failure to assign the responsibility to an individual or department, and sometimes just from the willingness to bet against the event and save cash.

Business package policies are inexpensive and rather comprehensive tools that should be contracted by all companies with any assets to measure and protect. A typical beginning package for a small company costs about $4 thousand a year, and covers a number of forms of liability both premises and product as well as employee use of self-owned cars for work, theft, employee dishonesty and more. There is usually a small amount of business interruption insurance in the standard package, and more protection can be added at a cost. Reading the list of protections is both impressive and frightening, since most of us never think of such risks, and it is overwhelming to have them pointed out in one reading. Conversely, the list of excluded protections is equally frightening for the same reason. We do not think of these unless someone points them out.

I believe my former software firm was responsible for one such exclusion that used to be a standard part of such policies. (Sorry about that.) With almost 250 employees, 26 of whom were application programmers, it was important to back up the work of these programmers each night, and an employee was tasked with just this each evening after midnight. Each night's backup would be carefully marked and the rotated between offsite and on-site locations in a series of steps so that backups of a day, two days, a week and a month were all available both on site and off site. Did I fail to mention that for more than a year we never tested whether the backups actually contained good data? It seems that a change in the operating system on the server we used for development was made that changed the way backups were cued, and our backup person was unaware of the procedural change needed to accommodate this. Came the inevitable day of the massive head crash, I quickly heard of the problem and the fact that all 26 programmers were standing by waiting for the backup to be restored, expecting to lose the partial day's work.

And the first backup from the night before was blank. As was each subsequent backup, on-site and offsite. It took weeks for the team to assemble code from various sources such as customer sites, beta test locations and demo machines. Then it took another several weeks for the programmers to come back up to speed rewriting patches and programs in a frustrating recreation of weeks and more worth of previous work.

I tasked our accounting department with collecting and calculating the costs of the labor lost, which was the only real claim for business interruption to be made as customers were unaffected by the problem. The cost came to well over $100 thousand, and a claim was filed with the business package insurer. After a short negotiation and quick audit, the insurance company paid $108 thousand to settle the claim. In the following year's renewal policy, I noticed a new page in the exclusions section, excluding for the first time data losses from failed backups, no matter what the cause or where the fault. As I recall, the year was 1987. Either we were the first to make a significant claim under this previously covered portion of the policy or one of several that did so in that year. Either way, you have me to blame for one more of those exclusion pages that overwhelm such policies today.

61. A worker compensation policy is not optional.

This is one that early stage CEO's are almost universally unaware of. Most every state requires that any company with employees be covered by a policy of insurance against claims by workers for injury on the job, or worker compensation insurance. Many states has privately owned but state-overseen state insurance funds for this purpose, and of course a number of private companies offer such insurance alone or along with business package policies.

In this increasingly litigious employment environment, it is mandatory for a company of any size to maintain worker comprehensive insurance. I have experienced incidents of claims that seemed quite minor on the surface where the employee was able to claim and receive large payments, sometimes over extended periods, for carpel tunnel injuries, slips and falls, neck injuries and more. Claims worth half a million or more are not uncommon. It may seem like an employee's lottery win to management, but the fact of the insurance award is real. In most states, the CEO and other executive owners of the corporation may be exempted from the policy and the costs reduced accordingly. Also, each employee is classified according to job performed, with some drawing very high premiums relative to others. With your agent's help, you should be very careful to place employees in the proper but most advantageous class for the sake of the policy.

Also, you will find all insurers asking for an estimate of gross payroll costs in advance of each policy year. At the conclusion of each year, before renewal, the insurance company will perform an audit of your payroll and bill the company for underestimated amounts, or credit the company for overestimation. These audits are often merely by telephone to your bookkeeper for small companies, rising to physical audits of submitted documents or in person for larger enterprises. Treat such policies seriously. For a reasonable cost, they protect against the strangest and saddest of employee-based corporate liabilities.

62. Employee first, company last, states the law.

Almost all laws dealing with employment are designed to protect the employee, not the company. Minimum wage laws, workplace safety, independent contractor tests, minimum hours required for benefits, worker compensation insurance requirements and more are examples of such laws. Notice that every poster that is required to be displayed in a company public area (usually the lunch room) is posted for the benefit of the employee to inform him or her of rights granted by law. To most entrepreneurs, this often leads to an event whose resolution by a governmental agency or even a court seems unfair and illogical. Issues that seem clearly based upon ineptitude morph into age or gender-related epic battles that most always end poorly.

So my advice is simple. Recognize the realities of the times, and do all possible to protect the company by documenting behavioral or skill related problems to the employee file. Hold regular reviews for all your employees right to the top. (The chairman reviews the CEO, and if there is no separate chairperson, then the CEO should ask an outside board member to do so.)   Encourage reviewers to be accurate, not just polite, in documenting areas of concern.

This is not to counter the advice of insight number 27, "Fire fast, not last", since every CEO should shoot for "A" class employees and not tolerate underperformers over time.

63. The 18 month rule.

It can take 18 months from initial concern about a critical employee to getting a replacement up to speed.

This insight is not mine, although I have experienced it several times with key employees since becoming sensitive to the concept. An old friend, Dick Tanaka, gets credit for this one. He observed that the process we follow to be humane in our handling of underperforming employees, manage the risk of future lawsuit, finally then move to separate the employee, define the open position, recruit the candidate, train the new hire and count the new hire as up to speed in the job can take all of eighteen months.

That is a shock in so many ways. First, the costs for underperformance are both tangible and intangible, with lost revenues, lost opportunities, lost savings and loss of productivity from low employee morale difficult to estimate. There are those in the recruiting industry that have attempted to do so, and depending upon the size of the company and the position replaced, seeming to settle upon astronomical lost costs that overwhelm most of our ability to understand. All of us will admit that, looking back at a failed employee hire, the costs were well beyond the payroll cost for the individual.

Perhaps this is a good time to speak about senior managers that are well-entrenched in the organization but are underperformers because the organization has passed their ability or span of control. We will explore this in detail in a future insight, but it is important to note the trauma of separating an old friend or close associate, or even a family member. There are few good rules for conduct in these instances, other than honesty in pointing out the problems, and doing everything possible to preserve the individual's dignity.

Early in the rapid growth phase of my computer software company, I hired an excellent, IBM-trained vice president of sales to further growth and begin our international expansion. He did so with gusto, and for several years was directly responsible for our growth into a total of 29 countries, including establishment of six foreign subsidiaries. Annual growth in revenues was between 50% and 100%, amazing and exhilarating. But he had a habit of bellowing out at underperformers, bullying others to get his way, and doing so in ways that rubbed all other managers the wrong way as he dominated meetings, and made it difficult for others to contribute. Surely a result more of his urban New York upbringing, I put up with these character traits as the cost for his amazing performance. And you might guess that, as his superior, I did not experience any of the threats to my job or dignity that apparently all others did.

I received a call one day from one of my country managers, stating that he and all of my senior managers would be at a meeting room in a nearby hotel the next evening at 7.00 PM, and that the vice president of sales, presently in the air traveling to the very country where the manager was to meet him, was not to be present. I was shocked and disoriented, a CEO with no idea of the urgency of the situation that was developing, since there had been no warning. Fourteen people, including the country managers and all the vice presidents, were to be there. I immediately called an industrial psychologist I knew, asking him to be at my side during the meeting to listen and interpret the mood of the meeting. (I have an industrial psychology educational background, but could not count upon myself to be completely objective here, of course.)

We walked into the meeting at the appointed time. Apparently the meeting had been going for some hours. Everyone but the sales VP was present as anticipated. As the psychologist and I listened to one after another of these, my most senior talent minus one, describe the assaults to their very souls, the affronts to their self-respect, the hobbling of their ability to perform, I was overwhelmed. There had been comments from some of these individuals in the past, but never voiced as an orchestra, and never with evidence so overwhelming and irrefutable. As the presentations of each concluded, my senior-most VP stood and stated calmly that if I would not remove the affronting individual, each and every one of the people present had agreed to resign. Now that's an act of desperation or defiance rare, perhaps unique.

I asked for a few minutes to confer with my associate. You might guess that it took less than that. As we returned to the room, I turned to the psychologist, the only third party in the room, and asked him to give the group his candid response to what he had heard. As I recall, he stated quite clearly that in many instances he is hired to repair relationships at senior levels in companies with such problems, paying special attention to coaching and training the offender, sensitizing him or her to the traits probably not noticed in self. But, he stated, as I recall, "This one is for the books." He had no advice other than to just do it and now. Of course, I had come to the same conclusion, even though at least in the short term, sales growth would suffer.

The rest of this story, if I took the time to tell it, would deal with the humanity of this next step, and retention of the dignity of a superior performer in all ways but one in his management abilities and in dealing with contemporaries and subordinates. I recalled him immediately back to corporate headquarters, and fired him after discussing the reasons with care, negotiating a reasonable separation package. The culture of the company thrived, and I could feel a collective sigh of relief from people even far below the level of senior management. And, although we have little contact after all these years, I have remained friends with this superior performer to this day. He understood, acknowledged the personality trait that failed him as one that had haunted him in his past, and became part of the solution once he and I had all of the facts on the table. It is a story that is extreme, relies upon one fatal character trait, but in other ways probably could match one or more of your own stories to tell or someday to experience.

64. Never run out of money.

Money in the bank is like oil in the car.

This is such an obvious observation that you should think that it does not rise to the level of an "insight". Yet, there is sage advice behind this statement that I could not ignore placing it right in the middle of these insights.   As an executive, you have many ways you are pulled every day, both tactical and strategic. But when money is the issue, your time, energy and focus are drained from other important areas of the business.

Running out of money is not always synonymous with "going broke". Many great businesses in their growth periods find themselves stretched for cash.   If fixed expenses, especially payroll, are paid out before cash is received from services or shipments, the company is financing its growth with ever-increasing working capital needs. Without remaining availability from a bank line, many businesses are stretched to the limit just when they seem to be doing better than ever. This is one interpretation of *"It takes money to make money"*, although that statement was probably created to describe new investment opportunities.

Speaking of which, those companies with cash in the bank and cash available are the ones to scoop up the bargains, from suppliers and in acquisitions especially during tough times.

But the most important lesson to learn is that cash is the great lubricant for businesses. Without at least a month's working capital needs on hand in the form of cash, receivables that will be cash, or an untapped credit line as a fallback, the CEO should worry over cash flow issues on a daily basis. Any disruption to the tedium of daily activity from weather, disaster, revenues slowdown or product problems will stress the company infrastructure if there is not a cushion to use during such times.

Stress of this type always forces senior management to lose focus upon strategic issues and drop into day-to-day tactical mode.

I find it a great thrill to consult to companies and their senior management when they have plenty of "firepower" (extra cash beyond needs) for acquisitions and strategic initiatives. It seems that the first subject that comes up in such assignments is the health of the competition. Such bargains; so little time.

Running out of cash denigrates the very value of a business, reducing greatly any bargaining power with suppliers or acquirers. A company that otherwise might be valued at twice book value, 1x revenues, or 10 times earnings will be valued at a lower amount by potential acquirers knowing that the company shareholders are in a tough position and management hungry for leverage and a little more sleep at night.

Never run out of money, even at the expense of slowing growth for a time. A fast-growing but undercapitalized company is not highly valued in an acquisition. For early stage businesses worrying over dilution when faced with an offer of more money than they need, the professional advice is most often to take the money and suffer the dilution because the money may not be available if needed later.

Cash is such a powerful inhibitor or driver of growth that management of the corporate cash is as important as strategic vision, and perhaps over time a good indication of the success of that vision to drive profits.

65. When cash is tight, slow its flight.

We have discussed *why* never to run out of cash. This insight delves into *how* never to run out of cash. There are four basic ways to increase the cash position of a company: inject cash through borrowing or investment, decrease spending or payments on debt, increase efficiency of operations, and increase revenues or advance payments from customers.

Even before examining the tactics of cash flow management, we've got to acknowledge that you never, ever should slip on payment of payroll taxes. The temptation to do so in tight times is tremendous, but the liability for such taxes are personal to senior management as individuals and cannot be waived or negotiated away. I advise all of my companies to use an impressed payroll service, one that takes the taxes from your bank account along with the net payrolls each period. I have a story about this for later in this insight. A close second for the same reasons are sales taxes and income taxes. Both of these take a bit longer for the appropriate authority to move to freeze accounts because the processes of doing so are more involved. But all forms of tax must be paid to avoid catastrophe, if not merely avoid 25% penalties.

Let's examine decrease in spending first. There are several classes of obligations and several types of providers within each. Assuming that the company is not already on the "cash only" list from materials suppliers requiring payment to those just to keep the business flowing, then when cash is tight, payments to ongoing providers of necessary services or products must rise near the top of the list. If there are several alternative suppliers of the same service that regularly deal with the company, then you have more power in lengthening payments to one. Calling vendors when payment is due but missed is always appropriate and will buy the company time and good will. But promises made must be kept, even if the amounts of payment are small. Some people advise that a company make small payments of any size to most all vendors, stating that these will keep the wolf from the door during tough times. I agree, but spreading the cash prevents making significant payments to those vendors needed most for continuing operations, and the balance is worth careful consideration.

In general, next in line are those that charge stiff penalties for late payment, including landlords and credit card companies. Often last are the lawyers and accountants who protect you and help you to plan your recovery, only because they above all others are vested with you in your recovery and success.

Accelerating revenues comes next. Close supervision of delinquent receivables is time-consuming but absolutely necessary. There are statistics that show clearly that the likelihood of payment drops quickly as receivables age beyond terms. And I've seen many company receivables clerks do a stunning job of collecting right on time by calling a few days ahead of time to check on the progress of a pending payment.

Thirty years ago, I stretched to buy a new home for my family that was above my ability to borrow at the time, but a bargain in a fast-rising market. My solution, aside from a first and second mortgage, was to call a number of my best customer CEO's, explain the problem-opportunity and ask for early payment of receivables. I promised each and later delivered a boatload of extra value for that evidence of good faith. As I recall, every one of the CEO's agreed to advance payments, and I did reward them with extra services. What may have seemed as a sign of weakness turned into a long term celebration of mutual trust and respect among peers.

Many companies have recurring revenues, often billed in advance, for maintenance or other services. Merely sending out the invoices for each period's pre-billing up to a month in advance of the start of the period will accelerate cash flow considerably. Many companies ask for deposits before performing services. Increasing the percentage of a contract as deposit is often unquestioned by small to mid-sized customers. Large corporations, those probably most able to pay such deposits, are usually the first to push back, often quoting "policy", whatever that is, as the authority preventing compliance with such a request.

I promised a story about payroll taxes, and it is not a good one, despite the best of intentions. One of my companies where I serve as chairman used a payroll service company that impressed payroll taxes along with payroll employee direct deposits and remitted those taxes directly to the authorities. Well, almost. One quarter, the company just did not receive its copies of the quarterly reports. I had wisely suspected this payroll company already and had the company switch to QuickBooks Payroll at the start of the new quarter. It turns out that the two founders of the small payroll services company absconded with (stole) all of the taxes from all of their payroll clients from mid-May through end of June that year. Since no tax authority notified any clients during those weeks no-one was aware that the money was gone and forms never filed. Millions were stolen. It is now years later, and our company as well as others have double-paid all the taxing authorities those missing taxes, including interest, but with penalties waived. The two founders are in Federal prison and about five percent of the missing funds were recovered by the Justice Department and returned to the companies. So it seems that even conservative cash tactics such as using an impressed service for payroll can lead to disaster. Who knew?

Now we turn to the more pleasant issues relating to growth, and explore some of the areas rarely considered when the rising tide lifts all boats. Those of us who have experienced exhilarating growth have stories to tell that make it obvious that the thrill of the wild ride makes the effort more than worthwhile. But growth has its issues too, and it is time to explore these.

Chapter Nine. GROWTH.

Growing companies are the envy of competitors, the darlings of service providers and often the targets for investment bankers looking to cash in on success. But there are insights here that point out the traps you may experience during periods of growth, and it certainly is better to examine them in the quiet of today rather than after a disastrous encounter on the front line.

66. Demand pull – cost push.

Place your cash bets behind proven demand.

The term, "demand pull – cost push" was created by the great economist, John Maynard Keynes, to describe the two primary drivers of economic inflation. Demand pull: too much demand for a product or service and not enough supply cause a competition for the product that drives prices higher without increasing the intrinsic value of the product. Cost push: labor or parts costs increase, causing the product or service to be priced higher without adding intrinsic value. As a student of economics, I studied Keynes and his many theories of macro and micro economics, but this one kept returning to me as an excellent way to describe a completely different business principle.

All of our enterprises have limited resources, even the largest of the Fortune 500, and especially the smallest of competitors in a market. Most new product introductions are planned with a broad campaign aimed toward the whole of the marketplace, committing resources such as money and manpower to the effort. I have learned over the years that this may not be prudent. Instead, seeding various segments of the market, vertical niches, with focused attention in form of marketing and sales efforts, will quickly yield positive results from some niches and perhaps no interest from others. It is upon the moment of understanding which niches respond positively to the new offering that a company should push costs into increased marketing and sales efforts into those niches, concentrating fire power and overwhelming the niche, instead of making few waves in an ocean of broad opportunities and becoming lost in the process. To describe this, Keynes comes to mind. Push the costs into market niches where you seed your marketing, and experience the pull of customer demand as a result. *Cost push – demand pull.*

67. Hire ahead of need only when growth is stable.

Many companies have made the mistake of using the forecast to plan and executive hiring of new employees so that they could be trained and up to speed when the demand arrives. Although such a practice does add to overhead by bringing employees aboard before they become economic contributors to the bottom line, there is much to be said about service quality by having trained employees on the front line when the customers want and need them.

There are periods in any economy or industry segment when growth seems steady and there are few warning flags ahead. In such instances, it is much less risky for a company to execute its plans for spending in coordination with forecast revenues. But there are many more times in which the near term future is far less predictable, and when early hiring decisions may be just the wrong move, reducing flexibility and reserve resources. It is during such more common times, that you should consider using temporary employees to fill demand as needed, even if brought aboard a bit early for pre-training.   And increasingly, there are off shore service providers able to contribute to production and service, expanding and contracting at will, with some sacrifice in control and sometimes in quality.

Further, a company suffers in its reputation with its employees when hiring and firing in short cycles to meet short term needs, unless those brought aboard are hired as temporary or seasonal workers. Every employee wants a stable work environment and does his or her best work in a culture of mutual trust as to continued service as a reward for good work. Constant interruptions in the chain of command, changes within the ranks and threats of impending layoffs together combine to form one of the greatest impediments to efficiency and a strong corporate culture.

68. Never use short term borrowing to cover long term debt.

This insight is one that is so important to the continued health of a growing company that it cannot be overstated. First, let's be sure we know what is short in term and what is long in term. Long term debt is taken on for the acquisition of fixed assets such as equipment, cars, facilities and acquisitions of companies or their assets. Short term debt is often composed of accounts payable to the trade or employees for expenses, payroll liabilities, accrued but unpaid vacations, customer deposits, and the portions of any loans due to be repaid within one year.

Asset-based financing is common for companies with accounts receivable and / or inventories. There are numerous lenders engaged in this practice, including most business banks. Typically, companies may arrange to borrow between 70% and 80% of those non-government receivables that have not aged past 60 days from invoice, up to a maximum amount, or "credit line".   Other companies have both the creditworthiness and relative size to be able to borrow from private and banking sources without collateral, with unsecured loans. Many of these lines of credit require that the borrower "clean up the line" for one month out of every year, that is to be out of debt with the lender for that period to prove to the lender that the need for the cash is not permanent, used like a long term loan.

Numerous companies have gotten into trouble by using the easy availability of these short term lines of credit, meant for rising and falling working capital needs, to make payments upon long term obligations such as asset loan payments when due. And worse, some even purchase assets such as equipment with money from short term loans. Matching the term of a loan with the life of the asset is an important business principle. Receivables are assets for only 60 days for the purpose of these lines of credit, and the available line can be reduced automatically as receivables reduce with payments by customers or aging beyond 60 days. We all expect new receivables to be added to replace these, but a cyclic business; a disruption in the general economy; a reduction in the company's revenues would each contribute to a reduction in the amount available for such borrowing. To avoid the coffin corner of an over-borrowed asset-based line with no cash for working capital, remember that short term borrowings such as these should never be used to pay any long term obligations or to purchase fixed assets.

69. Growth calls for more cash, not less.

Here we must do a little math calculation together to make a point. Assume that your gross margin from sales is 50% for ease in calculation. Assume 30 days to collect receivables from completed work, and 30 days to complete the work. Finally, assume a fixed overhead equal to all of the remaining 50% of revenues, just for the sake of making this point. Zero profit. Now consider an increase in your revenues from $1 million a month to $1.5 million, the extra $500 thousand to be billed in 30 days upon completion of work. During the first 30 days, you pay out over that period $750 thousand, the fixed overhead and cost of sales.

That's $250 thousand more than last month, putting you in the hole. You bill the $1.5 million on the 30th day and start the clock, waiting 30 days for receipt of the cash. During that time you receive the $1 million you billed the month before but pay out another $750 thousand in overhead for the following month. Where do you sit at the moment before collecting the $1.5 million billed last month? You are down an extra $500 thousand beyond the breakeven amount when you were billing a steady $1 million a month and paying out 50% for cost of sales and 50% for pre-ramp overhead. It took your company finding or funding $250 thousand a month for two months to finance an increase of $500 thousand in revenues. Surprise? Most managers are. If the growth continues, the amounts needed just increase and increase, until fixed overhead is no longer such a large part of revenues (growing more slowly than revenues), and perhaps margins increase with buying power and efficiencies of mass production.

With an asset-based bank line and a limit far higher than current need, a company can borrow against those receivables and eliminate at least the second $250 thousand of cash needs, since the receivable "pledged" for the bank line increases by $500 thousand. Most companies have little headroom in their asset-based bank lines, and such expansion of revenues can be accommodated only for awhile before the line is borrowed to its maximum.

Growth requires its own unique form of working capital cash planning. The mere fact of rapid growth is not enough to create capital within most organizations until the growth becomes more stable and receivables collections catch up with costs advanced to the various resources to "buy" that growth.

70. Forecast your cash position to sleep more soundly.

In the past insight, we created an example to demonstrate that it truly takes money to make money; that growth calls for increases in working capital. The example we crafted proved that companies can easily find themselves strapped for cash during periods of rapid growth as well as in downturns.

There are many techniques and time horizons for forecasting cash. For those companies with constant billings to customers during a month, and for those with extra large fixed costs such as payrolls at periods during a month, it is important to begin the discipline of the 13 week rolling forecast as a tool for finding and planning around short term cash problems. Each week, the actual cash position is updated and the past week dropped from the forecast and a new week added. This format is much more relevant to management that a monthly forecast when cash is tight, allowing for weekly planning in advance. In addition, and perhaps in place of this, for many more stable companies, a monthly cash forecast is appropriate and serves as an excellent planning tool for arranging any lines of credit or extensions of payment to suppliers over the month's time.

I've experienced periods of failure to plan short term cash needs, finding myself worrying over daily cash flow, and draining energy and focus from strategic issues. And I am sure many of you who have been in growing businesses have had this experience as well. For those of us who have lived through the worry of arranging for (or passively hoping for) cash to cover the next day's needs, this insight is a lesson learned. Even if accurate cash forecasting highlights a coming problem, the element of time and elimination of surprise both work to reduce the drain upon management, and allow for time to plan for ways to increase cash flow systematically. (See insight 65 for a few ways to do just that.)

71. Contribute to A-M-D, or support someone who does.

- **A.** Accumulate or acquire (product line, breadth of services)

- **M.** Marketing or merchandising (expert and diligent use of resources)

- **D.** Distribution (adding channels and reinforcing relationships)

Let me credit CEO Erik Hovanec for this one, whether he originated it or recast it from his past. As his chairman, I have watched him masterfully focus his 50 plus employees all toward a common theme aligned with the company's goals. The genius of this insight is that no employee is exempt, even those in accounting or human resources. Everyone supports the contribution to AMD in some way, or, according to Erik's challenge, should not be here breathing the air, taking valuable space and consuming scarce resources.

People in R&D, business development, purchasing or production all fit in to the "A" of the equation. Without constantly improving or increasing products to offer, a company today is quickly overtaken by its competition. Stagnant companies usually can trace their inability to gain market share upon the "A" area first, and management should pay particular attention to putting resources into this important focus of the company.

Without the "M", effective marketing and or merchandising, sales people and distribution channels quickly dry of leads and must fight for attention beside better branded competitors. Marketing is the area least understood, often least funded, and perhaps one of the most important within any company. Even with the best products or service, companies fail for the want of good marketing.

For many industries including those with Internet-based sales entities, you cannot have enough channels of distribution, the "D" in this insight. Some management will argue that channel conflict is one of the worst ways to lose the loyalty of distributor and direct sales resources. I'd counter that a cohesive distribution strategy calls for a coordination between inside and outside distribution resources by management, not a competition for customers using inside resources to compete with outside distribution. There are many ways to allocate or split a product or service in the marketplace: by size of customer, geographic location, market segment, or even agreed-upon rules to protect open competition between the distribution groups.

Sometimes, a company must create a unique brand to self-distribute in competition with other distribution resources. Many manufacturers have successfully created "OEM" labels for branded retailers wanting to distribute under the retailer brand, without disturbing other distribution channels. And many wholesalers have successfully created a new self-managed retail brand for direct distribution in competition with current retail distribution channels.

Focusing your entire staff on a simple, understandable set of functions in support of the goal is a masterful way to increase productivity, create urgency and measure contribution of individuals to the common good. Remember: A-M-D.

72. Celebrate each victory!

Growing companies give rise to many events that great managers will take advantage of to create and shape the culture of the company itself. Each new plateau in revenue growth, each time a month's orders hit a record, each large order from the sales department, all of these and more give rise to opportunities to celebrate publicly. Everyone in a stressful corporate environment loves to pause and relish the latest victory.

Each time our company would hit a new milestone, I would make a public announcement personally, then, with my payroll person in tow, walk the floors of the various company buildings handing out $50 or $100 bills to all employees as instant bonuses. You wouldn't believe how much people seemed to enjoy the boss' visits. The goodwill created and buzz that continued for days were well worth the small cost. Everyone got the message: growth is great, and everyone is treated equally in celebrating. Each distant or foreign office was included, although not often enough with personal delivery services. This is different from "managing by walking around", which requires no reason or structure other than the willingness to listen and learn from people on the line.

Many companies have a bell hung somewhere in or near the sales bull pen, rung each time a sale is consummated. Managers should encourage everyone within the hearing of the bell to stop long enough to applaud, reinforcing the unanimity of approval for each new sale.

Victories that shape a company's culture can take many forms. Years ago, an emergency phone call was directed to my office from our distributor in Australia. Their largest customer, Hamilton Island Resort, had just suffered a fire that destroyed the building containing their large minicomputer installation. No-one was injured, and there was a backup from the night before stored in a safe location. But there was no replacement machine in Australia, and each day that guests checked out without paying their bills amounted to a day where cash flow was at least temporarily reduced by at least $250,000, not a small amount as it accumulated. Simultaneously, we had a new machine with identical specs on the shipping dock for a Florida installation at a property whose managers were pushing the company for an instant delivery. I made the decision without pause to redirect the shipment to Australia that day. Then I immediately called the CEO of the Florida customer to explain. Not too happily, he acquiesced. Everyone within the company knew of the problem and of our instant reaction to aid our customer, even in the light of pressure from the Florida customer now back in line for shipment. We oversaw the successful installation in Australia the next day in a temporary building and our people helped key in data subsequent to the backup. Everyone knew from management's actions and their own efforts that the customer comes first, always. This story has a second happy ending. We engineered a rerouting of the Florida order a week later so that the computer to be shipped would be the 1,000th of its model. Before packing it in its large shipping crate, we held a party in the shipping dock for all employees, with streamers and cake and the world's largest greeting card – hundreds of sheets of continuous form computer paper, which every employee from software programmer to shipping clerk signed with a message of thanks and goodwill for the Florida customer's sacrifice. That week, we scored two great customer stories and more goodwill throughout the organization.

Victories come in many shapes, sometimes when least expected. Celebrate them all.

73. You are your company's moral compass.

Years ago, when I was CEO of my record manufacturing company in Hollywood, I happened to walk around the plant into the press room just as Bobby, one of the employees' favorite coworkers, was offering stolen merchandise to his fellow pressmen from a bag he was carrying. He halted, and waited for me to react, obviously caught in the act. Everyone loved Bobby, a hard worker and good friend. But I fired him on the spot; the only possible response to the situation presented me so suddenly. After initial shock, a number of employees came to me that day and said that they understood how hard that decision was, but that they knew it was the right thing to do.

You will find many times during your management years when such decisions are placed before you, requiring quick unwavering response to an ethical challenge to you or your company. How you comport yourself in these situations is absolutely the litmus test for how your company culture will reflect your actions. Take home company supplies for personal use? Your employees will surely follow your lead, no matter what the policy. Treat personal expenses at company cost, and your sales people will feel just fine doing the same until caught. Behave without regard for an individual's dignity when separating an employee who is a direct report, and other managers will feel little compunction to spend the extra time and energy softening their actions. Alter any accounting result for the sake of making a month look good, and your accounting department will get the message that GAAP accounting is just for show.

It is not easy to always be the moral compass for the organization, but it is the right thing and cannot be compromised. And you will continue to enjoy the stories of times taking the high road as retold to you by your employees over time.

74. Help your associates advance their careers.

We'd all like to retain our best managers and employees forever or at least for as long as possible. But sometimes our corporate wants and needs conflict with what is best for an employee and his or her career development. We cannot legally stand in the way of an employee resigning to pursue a dream, but we can leave a bad taste with that person and chip away at our corporate culture by not cooperating or even helping the employee move on. It doesn't take much to publicly wish a departing employee well, to throw a small celebration, to coach the outgoing person if asked, and to listen and receive fair criticism at the moment of the exit interview. And sometimes, the story that results is one that joins the ranks of super-tales, to be told again and again. Here is one such departure story I tell often.

Tom rose through the programming ranks to become the chief architect of my software company, with 26 programmers in his fold. The company had grown to 233 employees and served 16% of all automated hotels worldwide at that time. Each week, Tom and I would have an informal lunch and discuss issues that ranged far and wide. Tom almost always had ideas to contribute, particularly about marketing programs and opportunities.

One day Tom came to me and said, "I want to transfer to marketing. I am tired of programming." "But Tom", I protested," you are in charge of the family treasure. All of us depend upon you. Oh, the humanity…" Tom insisted, and nothing I could say would stop him from resigning, selling his home, and moving away. Five years later, I received an email from Tom. I keep that email in my leather note portfolio, carrying it with me wherever I go, pulling it out often to read portions to audiences during my workshops, or just for fun to fellow private equity investor friends. "Hello again, Dave," it began. "After looking around a lot, I have landed as employee number seven at a Seattle-based startup called Amazon.com." Tom goes on to extol the opportunities, describe his job in marketing with creative opportunities at every turn, and then… "My founder is in round two of capital-seeking, looking for increments of $100 thousand, and if you'd like, I'd be happy to introduce you…"

In one of the most understated several word paragraphs in history, I responded by email, "Gee, Tom. Good to hear from you. Keep me informed." After recounting this story, I then ask my audience to guess what an August, 1995 angel stage investment in Amazon might have been worth at the IPO, getting lots of range in the responses. The answer is $31 million. $31 million return from $100 thousand investment, or 310 to1. That story always gets a laugh as most everyone of us recalls the deal we didn't do, the investment we didn't make, the opportunity we shunned that turned to gold.

So you never know what good things will someday come, especially from talented, driven associates you nurtured but released into the wild when their time had come.

75. Never handle a paper twice.

We are not dealing with personal time management with this series of insights, except when it helps immensely to make a better manager of you and me. All of us have time management tips and tricks to help us get through the day. I have a mantra I try to live by, and it has helped me more than you know over the years. "Never handle a paper twice" may be extended to include reading and acting upon emails, messages, and any written distraction. It is human nature to filter through the stack or inbox, looking for the important items. And that certainly has defensible merits. But to find what is important, we usually have to at least scan a document or email, engaged for no less than a short moment and perhaps for the full reading of the document before moving on to look for important issues to resolve.

But there is good research to back up the statement that returning to a reading from a distraction causes the reader to lose up to 20% of his or her time in getting back to speed in mentally processing the document and its issues. By trying my best to adhere to the "never twice" rule, I quickly delete most copy-all emails not addressed to me, and all junk, but handle each personally addressed email as it opens in the reading pane. The exception is an email with an attachment that appears long and involved, such as an executive summary of a business plan. Those get shuffled into a separate inbox for later review, without exception. Using this policy, I get through my several hundred non-spam emails each day faster than I used to, and with more focus upon those with response required than if reading and returning to the issue at a later time, especially if not in the same sitting. Exempt emails from your superior and those marked as urgent, both of which should be either directed to a special handling inbox or culled out from the rest immediately.

Wouldn't you like to regain some percentage of your time with little or no effort? Try this one.

76. Sift your time through the filter of your vision.

All of us are pressed for time, always attempting to balance the overwhelming demands of business with the basic wants and needs of family. In earlier insights, we have examined the need for and care of your corporate vision, and how to develop and nurture that vision through to creation of a corporate culture, goals, strategies and tactics. Now we get personal.

Each of us makes many decisions each day as to where to spend the day's time. Many of our decisions seem to be made by others, with meetings scheduled requiring our attendance, the landslide of emails arriving hourly, emergencies popping up requiring immediate attention, and more.

The first thing to do as a senior executive is delegate whatever comes across your desk that is not directly relevant to your enterprise's and your own strategic importance to the company. That means teaching others how to do some of the work you have been doing, sometimes loading more upon another's full plate. We must assume first that your delegation effort is to those lower in the food chain. (They in turn must learn to delegate using the same filter, or if there is no next level, shed those items not in their strategic path.) Second, you have a vision for the company which you ask everyone to buy into as they plan and execute during their year. You should remember to take your own advice, and filter your activities through the needs of your vision, again shedding even more insignificant activities that cross your desk.

Who knows? These two filters when put in place might just give you back enough time to add a few enjoyable processes to your day, just for the lift they give. We can dream, can't we?

77. You are watched, mostly when decisions are tough.

If you have been in management or an entrepreneur long enough, you will have experienced the gray area of decision-making where ethics, the law, your needs and expediency all collide. This is the time when you are paid the big bucks, and when others aware of your plight will be watching most carefully. It is also the time when you demonstrate your true courage to your contemporaries.

I have a Ph.D. friend who teaches a graduate course in entrepreneurism at a local university. He uses the case method to place as many of these types of decisions in front of his students as possible each semester. And the responses from students are predictable. When faced with a gray area decision, the first response is to follow the letter of the law, the rules, the 'right thing to do.' The professor then injects one or more new facts into the case, and the students waiver, more and more as the new facts are analyzed, reducing their fervent enthusiasm for the "always right thing" stand. By the end of each case, most everyone has a position that has modified since the first impression. Then the professor reveals the action the company executive took to resolve the problem, often one not considered by the students.

Consider the case of the company with goods on the dock ready for shipment, a company with an accounts receivable-based asset credit line that is already at its limit due to the calculation by the bank of availability based upon current receivables. The rules for "pledging an invoice" as collateral for borrowing call for attaching signed shipping documents showing that the goods have been picked up by the carrier, at which point the title transfers to the customer and the invoice from the company is "good". The senior manager, whether the CEO or CFO or head of shipping, walks over to the location where the shipment sits waiting for pickup, complete with paperwork waiting signature by the carrier driver. The manager picks up the paperwork, and using a blank page inserted into the stack, signs in place of the carrier driver. He then pulls out the now signed company copy and returns to his office with just that copy in hand. Within an hour, the bank receives a copy of the invoice with the signed shipping document attached, along with a very standard request to borrow the 80% of the invoice amount. The bank clerk approves, adds the amount to the loan and company's cash account, and all is well. Or is it?

Invariably the students correctly point out that the company manager falsified a document, which surely is against the law since an invoice was pledged to the bank that was not represented by a completed shipment. After this discussion, the professor adds that he forgot to tell the students that the shipment made it to the dock minutes after the day's carrier pick-up and that payroll is due tomorrow and the cash must be in the bank today to cover the direct deposits. The only way to get that cash today is through the credit line borrowing, and after all, the carrier will pick up the completed shipment tomorrow morning. Now the students debate ethics against legality against pragmatism. Some hold their positions. A missed day of payroll is a small price to pay for even this small breaking of the law. Others state that the reputation of the company as a reliable employer is at stake, and that the employee loyalty will be shaken if payroll is delayed for even one day. The students divide somewhat evenly over the minor infraction.

Then the professor reveals that the shipment on the dock is only a small partial shipment but that the invoice that was pledged to the bank was for the entire amount of the order. Now the students debate whether the manager should be fired or the bank informed of the obvious falsification. And the professor adds that the manager in this case is the CEO himself.

Interesting enough, no student has yet suggested the Kubiachi Miru solution (*remember, Star Trek?*) where the CEO merely thinks outside the box or changes the rules. The CEO could have immediately called the carrier and offered a significant sum, say $500 for a quick custom pick up of the partial order, or called for the current location of the driver and found a way to load the shipment into a car or truck to meet the driver, or even plan to drive to the carrier's dock itself.

You get the idea. Decisions go from black-and-white to gray to black-and-white again, based upon relative knowledge of the facts and of course, the law. Just as a personal test, what would you do if you were the manager? Or if you were the shipping clerk observing this happening regularly? Or if you were the bank auditor discovering that this was a regular practice?

A CEO or manager's life is not simple. But there are lines, both ethical and legal, that just cannot be stepped over, difficult as the result may be. Each of us is tested in subtle and sometimes very public ways often during our careers. It is a simplification to state that the "good guys finish first", but looking back over long years of experience, there is a great deal of long term truth in that statement.

78. Bet the farm only when the crops are on fire.

This insight addresses the amount of risk you and your company are willing and able to tolerate over time. Most people believe that early stage companies should take risks aggressively because there is less to lose and much more to gain with each risky bet or decision. Common thinking goes on to address large, public corporations by expressing that the relative tolerance to risk is decreased, in favor of protecting the brand or financial health of the enterprise.

Either way, as in a Las Vegas casino, the numbers of times risks are taken directly affect the average outcome over time.   Take an extreme risk once, and you may win the bet. Your average is 100%. But for any sized company to continue to take major risks, the averages will surely catch up and the rate of success falls to the mean, which we will assume to be 50% of the risks result in failure. Depending upon the size of each risk, this may be entirely acceptable, as in small bets at the gaming table.

But this insight raises the ante by addressing those risks that are game-changing, those that "bet the farm." Occasionally, a CEO must make a decision that commits all of the corporate resources to a successful outcome. Using all of the company's cash and credit to produce a new product that is untested but shows every promise of success is one such bet sometimes made by CEO's of companies large and small. Automobile companies are famous for making such bets on cars that won't be on the market for 18 to 36 months from decision date, arriving at a time when gas prices and consumer preferences may have changed dramatically during that time. Some of those bets were unbelievably successful, such as the introduction of the Ford Mustang. Some were complete failures, such as GM's emphasis upon design and production of larger cars and SUV's even as consumers were voting with dollars for smaller, fuel efficient cars from foreign manufacturers.

We must assume that the auto company CEO's made their decisions to build based upon all available information, including consumer tests and market surveys. Many smaller companies just do not have the resources to do this in depth before committing resources which loom as massive to them toward a new product. Whatever the outcome, it is a safe statement that a decision-maker should commit major resources amounting to a bet of the business only when there is little alternative, that there is so much to gain that it overcomes the crippling loss that could occur. There are only so many times a CEO can get away with succeeding with such risky strategies.

79. Get to your goal by the most direct route.

There is more money lost in businesses today from inefficient processes than any other single area. Yet this is not a place where most managers feel comfortable deconstructing and rebuilding. Somewhere out there is a consultant or future employee (or even suggestions from present employees) that will provide the roadmap toward making your processes run more smoothly, more quickly and more inexpensively. As a byproduct, process quality is likely to improve as well.

No matter what your company produces, there is surely a more efficient way to approach the process. Start by carefully restating the goal for the process, such as "produce 500 quality units per day" and create metrics to measure the present output and quality (rejects or time lost) with this goal. Look inward, forming a "tiger team" from within your organization to define the steps presently taken to reach the goal, and make improvements in increments that can be put into effect and tested quickly. The best reward for those involved in improving a process is to receive the kudos from management and themselves for making dramatic improvements in their internal processes.

If internal resources cannot handle the solution, it is time to find an outside resource that can. Either way, someone must start with creating a map of steps from start to completion, breaking it down to measurable sized increments. Look first at whether some steps are creating a bottleneck or quality breakdown affecting subsequent steps (see insight 81 following this). If improving individual steps are not the solution, then scrap the process entirely and attempt to define a way to meet the goal through a differing route, such as outsourcing parts or the entire process, doubling the capacity of a segment of production, or redefining the goal itself.

All of these efforts will help you to better know the process to a degree you never expected to achieve. And meeting the challenge of improving productivity is a great morale lift for all, as well as good business practice for the company and management.

80. Create equity value with every step.

You may be an architect or doctor or other professional managing your business, knowing that the end game value of your client or patient list is small and not easily transferred to any buyer without attrition. In such a case, there is little advice here unless you think outside of your day-to-day profession and create a valuable leave-behind encasing your knowledge and experience that can be replicated and scaled to a large business – even if by others.

Most businesses fall into the class of those that can be sold someday to a willing buyer. Even small community service-providers can be sold to buyers hungry to get into a business already in revenue with a steady customer base. And many businesses are created with the express purpose of growing them in size and attractiveness to be ready to sell someday to create some degree of wealth for the shareholders. Accepting venture or angel money is to create a contract between the investors and the entrepreneur that the business will someday be sold or even go public to create an exit for the investors.

This insight covers all businesses and their management when thinking of the end game, as management should during each step in the process of building the enterprise.

What creates value in a business? Is your value proposition for an eventual buyer that you have some secret sauce that allows you to compete more effectively against competition? Do you already dominate a niche, no matter how small, that a buyer will someday want for itself? Do you have intellectual property that is valuable to you but might be more so to a buyer? These questions are just a few that I'd ask during strategic planning sessions each year to fine tune the value proposition for an eventual buyer. And I'd go further. Investments into the company, whether from new money or reinvesting profits, should be directed first into areas that will increase the value of the enterprise at the end game. You do this for yourself and your shareholders, and should be thinking of this regularly.

81. There is always a bottleneck. Sometimes it is you.

At many board meetings, I can be counted upon to ask, "Where's the bottleneck this month?" Senior management is usually prepared with an answer, and a good discussion of resource availability and application follows. Sometimes, the bottleneck is not so visible to the CEO. In those instances, I follow with: "Do you notice people waiting at your door, telling you that they were waiting for your response or decision, even if you were unaware of this?" And occasionally, this questioning leads the CEO to realize that he or she is the bottleneck through having created a hub-and-spoke decision process, with the CEO at the center of each process. Once the bottleneck is identified, the solution often comes quickly, requiring little if any board action as management focuses resources on the bottleneck to remove the latest impediment to efficiency.

There is a great book, *"The Goal – The Process of Ongoing Improvement"* by Elias Goddratt. The book was written to describe in simple terms the use of statistical analysis to remove bottlenecks in a manufacturing environment. I have used that book's lessons to teach process improvement to many types of businesses, including software development, supply chain management and retail fulfillment. I recommend that you drop everything and buy this book, read it, and if you find it as powerful as I did, purchase copies for your management team, followed by planned discussions among team members about removing bottlenecks and improving efficiency throughout the organization.

Think of the literal definition of a bottleneck in the business environment. Every resource behind the bottleneck is slowed from its most efficient pace until the resource ahead of it works its way through the constraint. In a manufacturing or production environment, that means people are stuck at their positions with completed work waiting for the process to move on. Or worse yet, more and more production is completed behind the bottleneck, only to sit as work in process, un-billable inventory of parts or services.

Behind or after the bottleneck point are people with too little to do, just like those in front of the bottleneck. But these people or machines have nothing to show for it, no way to accumulate inventory during the wait, just lost time waiting for the next process to squeeze out of the bottleneck. It is the worst form of lost opportunity within a production environment, all cost and no output.

Then there is the bottleneck itself, usually operating at maximum efficiency given the present resource size and ability to perform. If the resource is a machine and operator, would a second machine and operator remove the bottleneck and provide for a smooth flow? Add second shift at that station only? Add faster machine or faster operator? Allow fewer rejects from that point in the process? Attack the bottleneck from all angles to remove it.

The amazing thing about this process is the large amount of gain from focusing resources upon a comparatively small point of constriction - small based upon cost and time to fix. Work this question into you next management meeting and see if you are surprised by the results.

Next we turn to positioning of a company's products or services. There are rules, trade-offs and great competitive advantages in getting this right at the early branding and planning stage of a company's life. But it is never too late to create products or services to dominate a niche.

Chapter Ten. POSITIONING

There are many ways to position a company within a market in order to achieve maximum market share, maximize revenues, or maximize profits. In this chapter we will examine a number of insights directed at positioning your company, product or service to fill the gaps in larger competitors' landscape, and take advantage of the agility of smaller enterprises.

82. Faster is sometimes more valuable than better.
And doing both well usually wins the day.

This is one of those arguable insights, where both sides win. Dell is a great example of emphasis upon fast, creating a customized computer in 48 hours or less, bringing in assemblies and components just-in-time to make the assembly line. However, if Dell quality were poor and returns high, the company surely would not have survived on speed of response alone. If someone were to ask, "What is the secret sauce, Michael Dell?" Dell's response would be something like "Quality custom computers more quickly than the competition." And in this company example, both quality and speed are the critical factors in competitive advantage.

Think of McDonalds. Its reputation is based upon fast food in a minute, with quality that is acceptable but not discernibly above the competition. Or one of the instant auto service companies where an oil change is fast and inexpensive, but the number of inspection points far fewer than at a dealer location. Speed above quality. We have become a society not used to paying even a little extra for speed, but willing to pay much more for quality. How about the $14 hamburger at a restaurant, compared to fast food? We pay for the quality of product and service, happily defining our own tolerance for cost versus quality and speed.

So in planning for your niche to defend, one of the first decisions is between quality and speed. We will soon examine the entire gamut of pricing structures, but start with this one. It is fair to repeat that quality and speed together are the winners in this contest, not one alone.

83. Why buy IT? Why buy MINE? Why buy NOW?

What a powerful set of three questions. These are so succinct, so well defined, so precise that everyone in sales and everyone involved in marketing must be able to answer these three questions without pause, and convincingly. Turning these into statements instead of questions provides a framework for the sales presentation from the highest levels of collateral materials and marketing support, to the salesperson on the front line. It would pay you to work over this set of questions in a special session with sales, marketing and senior management in the room at once. It is that important.

Why buy IT? Can you, your sales people and your marketing staff answer this succinctly? Is your product or service one that responds to a customer need, real or perceived? This question deals with the offering in general, not yet with your version of the product. In general, there are three types of products or services: those a customer needs, those a customer wants, and those a customer believes he does not want or need. Your marketing and sales effort must be focused entirely upon making your product solve an urgent customer need. Sometimes, companies do this by creating demand where none existed before, such as for *Listerine* in the early days with a campaign to eliminate halitosis, the dreaded bad breath that consumers had no name for and did not think of as a need before that most successful advertising campaign. FedEx did not respond to a need for overnight package and letter delivery; it created the need with its clever advertising campaign. Car manufacturers used to make expensive annual model changes just to create a need in the minds of consumers who then viewed their present cars as obsolete. "What buy it?"

Why buy MINE? Product differentiation is absolutely necessary to make a sale when there is visible competition, as there usually is in any sale. Your marketing and sales people must know how to state clearly, with as few words as possible, the reason why your product best responds to the customer's needs. There is quite a difference between describing features, as many untrained sales people do and most engineering types almost always do, and describing benefits as a good sales person does. What the product does is less important that why the product solves the customer's problem, and how the product does so in ways obviously better than the competitor's product. This story should never be left to the sales person to make up, or each will make a different story for the purpose of a sale, not always aligned with the company's market positioning and rarely as precise and compelling as that created by professional marketers.

Why buy NOW? Without creating a sense of urgency, a sales person will have trouble closing the sale, allowing competitors another chance to make their case – often with the advantage of hearing the customer recount your benefits as he heard them. It is not a good place to find yourself, and is one where the odds of finally closing the sale drop considerably. Provide incentives for the sales person to use as needed to create the sense of urgency needed to push the customer over the line and commit now. Give him or her latitude for a discount up to a maximum percentage, dunning commissions by at least that percentage to make sure the tool is not used until needed. Provide a deadline after which the price will increase, the sale will end, the product will be re-allocated to another customer, or a tax credit will expire. Make the urgency clear with the sales person, so that no customer who waivers will fail to be offered something to make the sale now.

Recently, a roofing insulation sales person had my attention as he described his company's sale that would end the next Friday, and he made sure I understood that the Federal tax credit for such energy-saving home improvements would be applicable to this sale. He went on to state that the $4,500 cost would qualify for a tax credit (not merely a less-preferable tax deduction) of $3,000, or $1,500 for each of the two bundled services he offered. Something seemed very wrong to me about this credit, which I had recalled to be 30% of the actual amount paid. Because the sales person was not credible in this one area, I told him that I would check on the credit and call him a day later. Of course it took all of a minute using my search engine to figure out that he was attempting to apply his credit offer to the retail price, not the sale price, and twice for two products instead of once for the installation as a whole. I am sure other customers fell for this, but I was angry enough for this falsification of the facts that I called the sales person and not only declined, but read him the riot act in the process. *Why buy now?* Be sure there are no misrepresentations anywhere in the sales process.

84. Where there's mystery, there's margin.

Here's a phrase I created in the early 1980's to describe what I clearly saw as the last chance to make high margins on the sale of computer hardware to businesses. In the day of the mainframe and then the minicomputer, margins for manufacturers exceeded 35% and dealers were granted a 35% margin as well. Even with the usual discount of 10%, the margins on hardware were high, especially when applied to prices that exceeded $30,000 per sale.

In the early eighties, the IBM helped the PC become a tool of the office, and the product crossed over from use by early adopters to the mass market. Many other PC vendors flooded the market, including an uncounted number of "white box" manufacturers who created systems out of components imported from Asia. New retail channels popped up everywhere, competing for this lucrative, growing business segment. New magazines were rushed to market, thick with advertisements for computer systems and components at bargain prices. Many companies found internal employees able to install these computers and load software easily, without employing outside professional services.

And those of us depending upon the high margins from more expensive minicomputers found ourselves competing with these same PC's, now growing to be as powerful as the much more complex and expensive computers of just a few years ago.

Yet, there was one segment of the PC market that was not only growing but maintaining its margins as well as providing more professional services work than any other segment of the industry. Most of us could install a computer, but almost none of us could network that computer with others in the office or with other offices without equipment we did not understand, configuration tasks we could not perform, and training we could not offer. So we called upon our local value-added reseller with networking experience, often blessed with an earned certification by Novell or Microsoft. We paid high per-hour charges for professional services and unknowingly paid high prices for the networking equipment. But we were, as a class, happy with the fact that the computer and software costs had fallen so much that the networking costs were not an overwhelming portion of the computer budget.

Observing this, when in a planning session one day, I told my staff that we needed to find an area to defend our margins, one that still enjoyed the mantle of mystery to our customer base. Because, I said, *"Where there's mystery, there's margin."* We did find that niche and used it successfully for several years, in charging to certify and configure a company's self-purchased PC's so that they would work efficiently with our software systems. No employee of our customer company could do this because no employee knew our software and its requirements for database setup, multi-user security and more. We were able to add $1,500 or more to each small installation, and much more for large installations even though we no longer sold the PC hardware.

I told this story often in speeches to software and vertical reseller organizations, and the "mystery" expression stuck. Not only that, but I began to hear it restated back to me describing other industries in which similar progress had caused companies to search for a "secret sauce" they could defend.

It was only a small step to incorporate this into the strategic planning sessions for all companies that I later advised or served as a board member. And it still is important today.

I am an investor in a large home service company that specializes only in technology installations and repairs for the home and small business customer. With a fleet of Mini Cooper cars all marked with the distinctive logo and colors of the company, this fleet serves a growing need for fixing computer crashes, infected computers, networking issues, audio-visual installations and even fiber-optic installation in-home for a major phone-bandwidth supplier. They discovered the niche that many home owners and small businesses could not fill or understand.

Can you find a pain point where the customer cannot apply a solution without your help? One where the cost and value are both defensible in maintaining higher margins?

85. Pick your pricing niche carefully. Defend it.

There are five major classes or niches a company should examine and make its own in calculating positioning in the marketplace. They are:

- Price

- Quality

- Service

- Innovation

- Elegance

Companies that compete on price rarely compete against others who emphasize service or quality. Internet resellers have a better chance to combine price and quality than those with much more fixed overhead occupying a bricks-and-mortar physical presence in the community. But it is important for the image of the company to be known for one of the above attributes above others.

Some examples: Wal-Mart is known for lowest prices, often for identical merchandise found in other stores for more. But few go to Wal-Mart for quality brands, understanding that they accept Wal-Mart as the low-priced leader. Nordstrom's competes on service above all, quality second and price a distant third.   We enter a Nordstrom's store expecting superior service and know we will pay a price for this. Apple charges a premium for innovative products, with quality second and service third. Mercedes offers a premium automobile with its customers expecting luxury first, quality second, service third, and price a distant fourth. If Apple released a $229 notebook computer, it would damage the brand and reduce the value of owning an Apple computer in the minds of existing customers.

The very image of a company is influenced by this decision, as is every decision following the price positioning. In many markets, there are poorly defended niches, even markets with dominant players. Asus found this in the notebook and netbook market and moved in quickly to overtake all other manufacturers with low prices. It should be noted in passing however, that competing on price alone is the most dangerous strategy of all, since other well-capitalized players can easily join the competition merely by dropping prices upon existing products, of course at the expense of its previous positioning as described above. Asus was able to grab the mantle of price king while maintaining reasonable quality and even provide a bit of innovation in the netbook arena, worthy of applause by those of us market-watchers looking for examples of good strategic price positioning.

86. Plan for your 'every three million dollar crisis.'

Here is a phenomenon I discovered over time when dealing with many small start-ups in their early revenue period. A very predictable series of rotating crises seemed to befall most every one of these young companies. These became so predictable that I could accurately label them as occurring about every $3 million in gross profit (or revenue for service companies). By defining this in terms of gross profit, we can therefore include distributors with 15% gross margins as easily as software companies boasting nearly 100% gross margin.

There is a rotating series of predictable crises that most often reveal themselves like this:

At the $3 million revenue mark, the company often has grown from founders to about 20 employees, or $150 thousand in revenue (gross profit) per employee. Of course, venture-funded startups with long product creation times do not fit this mold as easily, often funded for long periods of losses with many more employees at hand in development positions. But at or around the 20 employee mark, the founders usually find that two things occur. The original management span of control is exceeded and management must be delegated to one or more middle managers to maintain efficiency in the workplace. Second, some of the original employees, occasionally one or two friends of the founders, are discovered to be falling behind as more professional employees show them up to be less competitive in their jobs. So management reorganizes the structure of the organization to fit the new needs of the growing enterprise.

At about the $6 million mark, revenues have ramped to the extent where the original product standards of quality are challenged, as is the speed and efficiency of customer service. Changes need to be made quickly to preserve the reputation of the company, adding a quality control function if not present, adding more QC steps in the process, addressing the number of customer service people on the line, creating longer hours to serve a larger customer base. Failure to respond to this predictable crisis quickly labels a company as a provider of poor quality, which seems to travel unbelievably fast among the industry, helped by competitors anxious to point out the problems. And once fixed, the perception of a fixed problem lags the reality by many months, making this a particularly tough crisis, common as it is.

At around the $9 million mark, the company suffers a most predictable cash crisis, one where the costs of growth in working capital and infrastructure creates the need for new sources of funds from investors, banks or asset-based lenders. If the company is not profitable, these channels for capital are not as easily tapped, extending the crisis and challenging the health of the enterprise.

Surprise. At around the $12 million mark, the company finds itself full circle, and in need of reorganization again along with a bit of house cleaning, pruning the poorer performers from the ranks. That's about at the 80 employee count, a time a little beyond when the company should have transitioned to a professional human resources manager to help solve this and future employee crises.

Do these sound familiar? They should, even if the dollar amounts are out of alignment with your experience, since some companies are funded well enough to skip the first financial crisis and some so efficient as to skip the first organizational crisis.

With this insight, you should be equipped to spot early signs of each crisis and plan around them in time to avoid the full impact of each in turn.

87. Stay current or the market will drift away.

Markets and competitors change. Are you being left behind?

Over the years, I have often heard the complaint from CEO friends that they have become so swamped by the demands of their growing businesses that they feel themselves further and further from the center of their industry, no longer at the forefront of information and competitive development.

It is a real risk for the successful entrepreneur that the daily demands of business make it more and more difficult to know the pulse of the industry, which becomes more and more risky as decisions are made and resources allocated to projects or products that may no longer be as attractive as before.

During the past several years, some very big bets have been made by large companies and well-healed entrepreneurs in old media, newspapers and TV stations. Although newspapers have a window in which to reinvent themselves by providing electronic delivery and TV the same by recasting into more niche markets through division of digital channels into niche-serving slices, I doubt that these bets will prove profitable in the end, because of the overwhelming availability of free media using the web. Were these companies and entrepreneurs out to a long lunch during the media transformation? Or do they know something all of us commoners do not?

88. Develop the "What if" question chain method.

One of the most valuable tools in an executive's arsenal is the use of the question chain in planning meetings or to analyze scenarios that might result from an action. The powerful words are "What if…" followed by an ever-deeper question that follows the possible results of an action, or a decision based upon the last "What if" question.

The beauty of this method is that it causes the person proposing the solution to think much more deeply than during the development process, unveiling many possible consequences to be considered before implementation of an idea or project.   When I use this technique, invariably the person on the other side of the question will at some point state, "I didn't think of that."

In a recent CEO roundtable, the executives discussed their experiences with the question chain. Several had revealing things to say about their experiences. One stated that he asked "what if" the U.S. dollar was to sink in value during the life of the foreign transaction. The subordinate had not thought of this carefully enough and had no protections built into the agreement or any strategies to hedge currencies. The net cost of such a failure to pre-think this event would have been in the millions, stated the CEO, but were successfully hedged against just as the dollar declined. Another CEO in the group offered his experience with the question chain relative to the availability of isotopes for his company's medical instrument customers in the event of political turmoil in the countries where the nuclear material was exported. As a result, his was the only company among the competition to continue to service his medical industry customers when just such an event occurred.

"What if" are two very powerful words when used together. Use them more frequently as you manage your enterprise.

89. It is satisfying but rarely profitable serving early adopters.

I am a gadget freak, often purchasing new technologies in their first release. And my closet is full of such gadgets, from early pen-based computers to early brick-sized cell phones to an electronic handwriting recognition pad received as a gift to test. These early dives into new technologies serve a purpose for me. They keep me at the leading edge of new development as it is productized, even before mass production. They allow me to preview new devices and technologies before release so that I might write about and speak about them in my "Tech Trends" keynotes. And they are always the center of attention with my tech-savvy friends, some of whom are in the habit of asking, "So what's new today" each time we meet.

The cost of such attention-seeking and research is relatively low for me, and certainly the reward of being sought out as a speaker addressing the trends in technology is enough in itself.

But I have been on the other side of the early adopter development process several times in the past, and can attest that it is great fun, but rarely profitable to be the first with any new product that requires simultaneously evangelizing or teaching the masses within the industry and marketing the new product offering. The costs in playing such a dual role are many times that of those in positioning a new product in a niche already opened by another. And statistically, the first product into a niche is very rarely the one to succeed.

Apple, for example, was nowhere near the first to introduce an MP3 handheld music player. I had owned several before the first iPod was released. Apple learned that their leverage was in the simultaneous creation of an easy-to-use retail music store for seamlessly downloading songs, podcasts and later applications to the device. It did not hurt that Apple always seemed to trump the competition in design of the product and the product's user interface too.

In 1986, while in the hotel technology business, I observed the back-room success of American Airlines with their new Sabre subsidiary and its creation of a "yield management" system to use massive data to project demand for an airline seat on a particular flight segment days and months into the future. I was not alone among hotel industry executives curious for more information. And Sabre was not talking to anyone about their magic potion. First Hyatt Hotels, then Marriott Corporation called me to their respective headquarters to consult with their executives on this subject under a non-disclosure with each. I became even more excited about the concept applied to the hotel industry. Both of those chains had very primitive modules in their respective reservation systems. Marriott called theirs "tier pricing". If a future date was already booked at 80%, then they would eliminate any discounts below 10% from the "rack" or standard room rate. At 90% they would stop discounting entirely. These elementary steps were in the right direction but very primitive.

So I set about partnering with a small group of MIT graduates to produce specialized decision software for the hotel industry using the "LISP" programming language, created just for decision-making, allowing for coding inductive and deductive logic into the software. I partnered with Texas Instruments, producer of a LISP computer, the TI Explorer. We designed and produced special cards for the TI that would allow Apple Macintosh workstations to be used, with their handsome graphic user interface. Then I designed what was then a ground-breaking new software system that could analyze tons of data from past guest stays on the same date a year earlier and other dates with the same day of week, add factoring for city-wide events on any future date such as pro football games and conventions, analyze the speed of increase in any night's future reservations, and much more. Each night, the system was designed to perform its analysis using real advance reservations data current to the moment, and run the data through a series of rules I wrote which could be modified or added to by local hotel management, to automatically make pricing decisions and automatically implement them. The system coordinated decisions between the reservations department which accepted individual or transient reservations and the group sales department booking groups at a discounted rate, allocating available rooms between each in order to achieve maximum revenue for any future date.

I found a willing test site in the Royal Sonesta Hotel in Cambridge, Massachusetts, whose management was thrilled to participate in an industry-changing experiment with new technology. The system was priced at $150 thousand, but we calculated that the average decision implemented for the 300 room property should be worth $5 thousand, making payback within an amazing 60 days if all worked as planned. Our company installed the system, integrated it with the Sonesta computer system which our company had previously provided, trained the staff, and began to measure the results after turning on the system in a live environment. In the meantime, we sold a second system to a large timeshare resort in Orlando for the same price. By agreement, Sonesta withheld payment until completion of the beta test period.

The industry's annual technology trade show came up during these tests. The industry was abuzz about this "artificial intelligence" system and its purported early results, and I wrote the cover story for the industry magazine about the system, and organized a panel composed of executives from Sonesta, Marriott and other chains to present and discuss this newest industry marvel. On the day and hour of the panel, it became obvious that the house was way overbooked. We agreed to repeat the panel later that day for the hundreds of people unable to get into the large room. We were a great success with a great, ground-breaking product.

And the next week we asked for payment from the test property, after sign-offs from all of its managers but the top one. The general manager was also an executive of the family chain of hotels. He called me in, along with several of the second level managers so enthused about the system, and stated, "This is nice, but I could do this work on the back of a napkin," shocking us all, and he refused the pay for the machine. I challenged him immediately. "Let's disconnect the system from influencing the reservation system for one week," I offered, "and let the machine calculate but not implement its decisions. During that week, you make your decisions each night on the back of your napkin. At the end of the week, we'll compare the effectiveness of each. If you agree that our system was more likely to positively affect revenues on those dates targeted, you pay for the system. If not, we'll remove the test system and find another home for it." He agreed. Management added a few new rules to the rule base and watched over the system each evening, anxious that there be no contest between this number-crunching wonder and a single manager's intuitive guesses.

A week later, I again traveled across the country to the property to meet with the same team and the general manager. We printed out the week's decisions, those not implemented. We presented our findings, and waited for the GM's response. "I did not bother," he stated. "I have no doubt that I could have done this better if I'd taken the time; but I was busy this week."

We could not argue with the money, even if we were right and all other managers desperately wanted to keep the wonder machine. So we removed the system. After all that great press, I realized that the industry just was not ready for such a leap, giving up authority to a computer, even if at least one major airline had successfully done so. I offered to repurchase the second machine from the hotel in Florida. After all, what company can maintain such a small number of unique systems?

I turned to Tom, our chief programmer (see number 74), and directed him to use as many of the features of the knowledge based (artificial intelligence) system as possible, but reprogrammed into our standard reservations module using our BASIC programming language. Tom's team did just that, perhaps saving 70-80% of the functionality even if none of the leading edge glitz. We priced the reduced "feature" at $8,000, and sold many over the years as mere add-ins to the reservation system.

After spending over a half million on the project (and receiving at least that in great publicity), I learned a lesson repeated here. *It is satisfying but rarely profitable to cater to early adopters.*

Finally, we turn to the end game, the goal for many entrepreneurs and investors. Selling the company at just the right time to a willing buyer at a good or great price is an exhilarating experience. We explore planning for that event and its aftermath in our last chapter.

Chapter Eleven. LIQUIDITY and BEYOND

If you took funding from outside investors to make your company a success, you made a pact to build the company in value and someday find a buyer for the business. Professional investors look closely at the entrepreneurs they finance, expecting to find sincerity in that promise. Many serial entrepreneurs hunger for the next opportunity to create a new business, with the rush that comes from the ignition and growth being their greatest reward.

There are many things you and your investors and managers can do to assure a greater likelihood of success in the ultimate sale of the company. And there certainly are effects upon you and others to consider during and after the sale.

This final chapter delves into these issues with a number of insights gained from tens of liquidity events over the years, and of their aftermaths for the various entrepreneurs involved.

90. Think of your exit as you commit your resources along the way.

Each decision you make to commit resources affects the future value of the business to some degree. Minor decisions, such as replacing employees who have left the company or equipment needing updating, are usually considered operational in nature, and unless the business is changing direction, not relevant to this analysis. But each commitment of resources of any substantial size for acquisition of new products, talent, even new companies, changes the value of your enterprise perhaps to a great degree.

Let's analyze the effect of a potential acquisition upon the value of your company. We must assume that you intend to sell the enterprise at some point in the future. There are many reasons a company finds to make an acquisition. New products, new geographic territories, elimination of a competitor, increase in revenues, consolidation savings, new talent, new distribution channels, and more are good reasons for considering an acquisition.

Given these possible goals in making a good acquisition, there is one overarching question that you should consider before making that decision to acquire a company. Know first that statistically, 80% of all acquisitions do not meet the intended objectives of the acquirer, making most all acquisitions risky. The question to study in your board meeting long before making any offer to purchase a candidate business is: "Would this acquisition add significantly to our enterprise value and attractiveness in an eventual sale?"

If the answer is "no", and there are other opportunities for the use of cash that would add value, it would be wise to allocate resources to those opportunities. After all, we are in business usually for the ultimate return we will someday receive from our investment.

91. There are three kinds of business buyers.

This is one of my favorite insights, since I lived this one in a positive exit from my computer business. Most people will tell you that there are two kinds of eventual buyers for your business: *financial* and *strategic*. A financial buyer will analyze your numbers, past and forecast, to the n'th degree, and calculate the price based upon the result, after carefully comparing your numbers with those of others in the same and similar industries. The object of a financial purchase is to negotiate a bargain, capable of payoff through operating profits or growth over time, or even of immediate profit from arbitrage – knowing of a purchaser that is willing to pay more for your company if repackaged, or even with no changes at all.

A strategic purchaser is one that understands what your company has to offer in its marketplace, and how your company will add extra value to the purchaser's company. Strategic buyers look for managerial talent, intellectual property, geographic expansion, an extension into adjacent markets and more that will be achieved with the acquisition of your company. Such a purchaser usually is willing to pay more to secure this new leverage, understanding that the value of the acquisition is more than the mere financial value of your enterprise. Most investment bankers will coach you into helping them find you a strategic buyer, knowing that such sales are quicker, often less focused upon the small warts of a business, and yield higher prices than financial sales.

There is a third class of buyer I discovered first hand when selling my company - the *emotional* buyer. This rare buyer *needs* your company. He must have you or one of your competitors, and now. The buyer may be a public company attempting to defend decreasing market share and being overly punished by Wall Street. You may represent the only obvious way to protect against obsolescence from a buyer's declining marketplace, or failure to compete against others with better, newer technologies. You may be a most successful direct competitor, one that the buyer's sales people have observed jealously and nervously, sometimes even jumping over to your company as a result. No matter what the emotional focus, the buyer cannot continue to stand by and watch its business challenged so effectively. The price negotiated is not at all the critical factor in the emotional sale. It is the elimination of pain that drives the buyer to action.

I experienced just this phenomenon and profited by the added value in the transaction provided by an emotional public company buyer for my business. The potential buyer was a hardware company, well aware that margins were decreasing and that software companies, once considered mere vehicles to help sell hardware, were now becoming the central component in a sale, mostly because hardware was fast becoming a commodity as prices dropped. My buyer-candidate had previously licensed our firm as a distributor, a value-added reseller for its hardware. As we grew to capture 16% of the world market in our niche, we successfully migrated from the single platform of the buyer-candidate onto hardware from any of its competitors from IBM to NCR to HP and others. At the same time, the buyer-candidate realized that we had become its largest reseller. In one of many meetings with the buyer's CEO, I "accidentally" dropped the truthful fact that his hardware now accounted for only about a third of our hardware revenues, down from 100% several years earlier. It did not take but moments for him to realize that his largest reseller was giving his company only a third of its business, that his revenues were declining and ours increasing dramatically. Simple in-the-head math shocked him into the realization that, if he could increase our use of his equipment in more sales, that he could slow or stop the decline in his revenues and he could migrate into a more software-centric company, much more highly valued by Wall Street, which was punishing his company for its decline and coming obsolescence.

The resulting negotiation was rather quick and very lucrative for our side. It was the first time I had witnessed an emotional buyer, and appreciated the difference between "strategic" and "emotional" immediately. Ever since, I have been urging my subsequent company CEO's and boards to perform an exercise at regular intervals to seek out and identify future strategic and emotional buyers. We'll describe that exercise in the next insight.

92. List ten companies that could buy your business.

This is an exercise I perform with my boards no less than once every several years in planning exercises attended by the board and senior management, sometimes augmented with an industry consultant or expert from the outside.

Use a white board visible to the entire group. Draw and label four columns and ten rows. The columns: "Name of candidate buyer", "what they want", "what we want" and "likelihood".

Then in a brainstorming session, fill in the ten rows with the names of ten potential purchasers of the business, looking deeply for strategic and emotional candidates (see insight 91). Next, return to the list on the board and have the group do its best to divine what it is about your company that would most attract the buyer if it had perfect knowledge of your business and its resources. This could be your intellectual property, your geographic reach, your superior product, your management team, or perhaps your dominant position. Next, have the group focus upon column three, ignoring the obvious gain our company would make in liquidity to shareholders. List what the company would most gain in new resources from this acquirer. Would it be more cash for expansion, new intellectual property, better distribution, completion of drug trials, or more? And finally, have the group put a number in column four, estimating the likelihood of such a sale ever being consummated, with "10" the absolute highest and "1" unlikely to occur.

The magic of this exercise is not only in the organization of group focus upon the liquidity event and possible buyers. It is in revisiting column two of the chart. You will quickly note that at least four of the ten candidates, if each had perfect knowledge of your company and its resources, would want the very same thing from an acquisition. Whatever that is, it shines as the true core competency of your corporation, whether previously expressed or even recognized by management. It is in this area where I would redirect resources such as manpower and money, to build value more effectively and quickly than in any other area of the enterprise.

Occasionally, the insight gained from this exercise comes as a complete surprise to the board and management. And that is most rewarding to see.

93. Timing is everything in a sale.

I have saved this next story until now because it is one of my favorites, and certainly illustrates the point as well as anything I could devise from fiction.

First here is a bit of the background. The year was 1998. After presenting a "state of the company" report at a national meeting of resellers for a company where I sat on the board, I was approached by one of the audience members, complimenting my presentation and stating, "I have a problem. I've been offered $15 million for my company and my partner is suing me for all I am worth. What can I do?" I promised to come see him at his office the very next week. What I discovered was a contradiction that was too intriguing to ignore. The company of eight was engaged in web design, hot at the time. And yes, the partner had a valid suit, having been locked out of the business and denied access to decisions and accounting information. But the real asset became obvious at almost exactly 5 PM that day, when all eight stopped what they were doing and began using a tool they had licensed from a Florida company to find other Internet gamers to join them in playing intense first party shooter games over the 'net. The tool it turns out had been posted on the company's website and downloaded by over a million gamers. Over a million of these came to the company's game web site each month for new information and to form an early Internet game community. The company made little effort to charge for the software or community. Microsoft had just bought Hotmail for $9 per registered user; AOL had just bought ICQ for $40 per registered user. And here were over a million users, with no apparent value to the web designers, except as a community of friends with similar interests.

I did forget to tell you that on that day looking into the company's books I discovered that neither the company nor its founder had filed Federal income tax returns during the three years in business, didn't I? And there were other quite obvious problems, unattended to, along with the partner's suit hanging over their heads.

I immediately agreed to come aboard at no cost to clean up the corporation, deferring my investment until that was done. I negotiated a settlement with the partner for $100 thousand which I paid, then filed all of the overdue tax returns of various types, and cleaned up the books. Offering to reincorporate the game company as a new entity to avoid any more surprises, we negotiated 10% for my $100 thousand, with the remaining 90% for the founder. In addition, I loaned the new company $150 thousand for working capital. By this time there were not one but four million registered users.

Within three months, we easily obtained $3 million of investment at a pre-money valuation of $30 million. Can you begin to tell that this is a story of timing, and of the Internet bubble? Three months later, another investor company in the business offered to invest $3 million at a valuation of $60 million. Two months after that, a French game company offered $1.5 million at a valuation of $80 million. Of course we took all of these.

We now jump forward to February, 2000, 14 months after formation of the company. Another major competitor in the industry, directly competing with one of our investors, offered $140 million for 49% of the company in a combination of equal cash and stock in its public entity.

Fast forward a month to a meeting between a senior executive of the buyer, our hero the entrepreneur, our corporate attorney and myself. In planning for the transition about to take place, the executive stated to the entrepreneur, "You know, we are buying only 49% so that we do not have to roll your losses into our income statement; but we do expect to make the decisions as if a majority owner." Our entrepreneur, engorged with the year's effortless value increases, turned to the executive without a pause, and said something to the effect of "Hell no! We can make this company worth a billion without you!" And so, a mere month before the crash of the Internet bubble, the buyer withdrew the offer. And, even if some of us were more than unhappy, we went back to the work of building the company value. And a month later the bubble burst.

It took almost four years to sell the company for over $60 million, not at all a bad outcome for us founders and the early shareholders. And I do need to note that the entrepreneur in the meantime became a model executive of a growing company, much more mature and understanding of market forces than that fateful day in February, 2000.

Could I have found a better example of "Timing is everything"? The lesson: Look for cycles in your business and in the marketplace. There are natural high points in one or both that may not be obvious until looking back. But they occur often enough to watch for and take advantage of if ready to make the run for a liquidity event.

94. A successful exit is a great measure of a good journey.

I've been involved with well over a dozen successful exits over the years, some of them with monstrous gains, some more modest. Then in addition, there are the exits that returned some portion of capital, but nothing more. And finally, there are the sad exits that were complete write-offs for the investors, regaining some portion of note-holder or creditor money in the process. I can tell you with great enthusiasm that the high gain exits are by far the most enjoyable in every way. There's almost always a closing party where the board, prime investors, attorneys and investment banker all get together to celebrate the victory. It is an exhilarating ending to a great journey. The entrepreneur, whether remaining to the end as CEO or not, is celebrated for his or her prescient timing, great vision and excellent execution of the plan. One such celebration was even characterized as "We stuck the pig!" - the overly enthusiastic celebration of an outcome larger than expected.

But I cannot recall ever attending a closing dinner for a sale in which we returned only a portion of the investor group's money. In fact, I don't recall any formal post-sale meeting at all; even to digest the lessons learned from the entire experience, a missed opportunity for all.

And there is the sad truth of the large percentage of early stage investments that die an unceremonious death, often with the entrepreneur-founder left with a bitter feeling that "if only" there had been more cash invested, more co-operation from board members, more time to get to market, more of something, then the outcome would have been much better for all.

Of course the successful outcome is preferable for all. But more importantly, it marks a passing of a successful journey by a team first formed by a visionary entrepreneur, usually attracting smart money from good investors, who together effectively planned growth and finally a great exit.

Whenever those forces come together, celebrate them and the team that brought them all together.

95. Time does fly when you're having fun. Lighten up for maximum lift.

Have you ever noticed how slow time passes when you are in a troubled environment? Conversely, sometimes you look up at the end of a great day and wonder where the time went. Over the years, I have discovered that the difference is not just applicable to the good times, but to the environment, created by the senior executives, that filters throughout the organization. Every time, a corporate work culture encouraging humor causes employees to enjoy their work, spend more time with associates, and laugh many more times through the day.

At one point in our mutual careers, my brother located his growing architectural practice just a mile from my record company in West Hollywood, California. I would visit his office and immediately notice an atmosphere of "joyous creativity" throughout the organization. Every cubicle was decorated with whimsical drawings, posters, kid's creativity, and more. As I walked through the facility, I could hear laughter emanating from cubicles, almost constant as a background song of simple joy at work. Those visits were wonderful times to recharge my batteries, and I was not even a part of the company. Imagine how they affected the attitude and creativity of those working there. Think of how clients loved to associate with their counterparts in such an environment.

Try as I could to reproduce such an environment, my company was too spread out, the background noises of manufacturing too loud to make the same environment possible. The best I could do was touch individuals and small groups with that same joy of the journey, adding humorous opportunities for lightening up as often as possible.

But after all these years, I will never forget the magic of that architectural office, and how much everyone there wanted not to let it ever slip away.

Take every opportunity to lighten up, to ease the often-self-imposed pressures of constant work, to unlock more of the creativity of your workforce through the use of appropriate humor. What a lift that brings.

96. Create stakeholder loyalty when times are good.

There are several times when stakeholder loyalty is tested to the limit. For employees, a late or missed payroll is the ultimate test of corporate loyalty, divorced even from an employee's ability to make do without a paycheck. For investors, a subsequent down round at a lower valuation than the last, or an exit opportunity at a loss are all opportunities for the affected stakeholder to show a side that can sometimes shock an entrepreneur or CEO. Managers almost always believe that stakeholders understand the pressures of the business and the circumstance of the present. The truth is that many employees merely make a simple pact: timely pay for time in service. If there is no closer connection to the corporation, when times are tough for any reason, it is these employees that make it tough for management to gain understanding and consent for actions that must be made such as missing payrolls, making layoffs, or abandoning pre-announced plans. And it is that disconnected employee, usually one or more of the better performers, that starts looking for a job when times look bad for a company.

Sometimes a secondary fund-raising effort leads to a lower valuation than the last. Although the investment documents from the previous round call for each investor group to vote as a class for or against new rounds of funding, in a contentious environment even a company in desperate need of new funding may find itself warring with its investors. I have seen investors allow a company to die, rather than suffer the massive dilution of an offer by a new investor.

And I have seen good offers from buyers of a company blocked by investors whose vote is needed to enable any such transaction, usually because these later investors would have a less-than-stellar exit with the sale, even if the founders would make out extremely well. That one hurts early investors and founders more than perhaps any other action by investors.

The message here is simple. By keeping stakeholders close with constant information as to the progress and even stressful setbacks, and by never withholding bad news, stakeholders will be in a much better position to understand necessary actions by senior management, and accede to decisions made in the best interest of the company, even at the expense of self. This kind of loyalty is never created during the bad times when everyone is thinking only of protecting self. Take advantage of the good times to build such loyalty.

97. Everyone wants to leave a legacy.

Be honest now. Have you ever thought of what legacy you'll leave behind? If you are an entrepreneur or CEO, surely you've thought of how you'll be remembered by your associates and stakeholders after you move on.

We've all heard the stories of tough SOB bosses that took advantage of employees, vendors, even stock holders. And such stories do get around. How many people who know those stories are willing to trust their next chapter to that person's next act? In my past, I made it a practice to hold exit interviews personally with nearly all separating employees, gaining insights from them they would not be willing to share while still employed with the company. And invariably, I'd end each with a handshake and the admonition: "I want us to part as friends. We never know how we're going to meet again, perhaps with the shoe on the other foot." I did not know for many years, until a most successful reunion planned by my former executives bringing back over a hundred past employees, how much that and other signs of respect and dignity for the employee-associate made our workplace rare and desirable.

I used to receive a list of birthdays for the next month from my assistant, culling the information from the corporate books spanning offices in many countries. Once a month, I would maintain the ritual of going to the local gift shop and buying enough birthday cards to fit each employee or associate. And once a month, while watching TV, I spend part of an evening writing personal messages to each birthday employee, recalling an event or complimenting a behavior or success. Such amazing accidental returns for such a small gesture. Even today, years later, I am met at industry events by former employees with a common refrain, "Our company was the best employer I have ever had, before or since."

That is a legacy you cannot buy, at a cost of acknowledging individuals with respect and personal recognition.   And what do I remember about that ten-plus year experience, among the thrills of rapid growth, great workplace, and great lucrative exit? Most of all, it is those personal moments of contact with former employees, each recalling with appreciation their time at our company.

98. Share your liquidity success with those who got you there.

Some companies have good, formal stock option plans with properly priced options set to reward all in the event of a corporate sale. Usually, the higher the ranks, the more the options held and therefore the greater reward at exit. If there has never been outside investors to organize such an option program, many CEO's never get around to creating a system for rewarding employees in a sale.

I found myself in such a situation upon a sale of my computer software company. There was no question that each of the five vice presidents had been greatly responsible for our success and getting us to the successful exit. Yet there was no formal reward in place other than the employee stock ownership program (ESOP) which was set to pay all employees for their accumulated shares at the exit. So I wrote into the final distribution instructions a surprise five figure bonus for each of the five executives.   Each was surprised, pleased and effusive.   Upon reflection, I should have given each even more.

99. Leave something on the table in a sale.

Isn't the goal of any negotiation to get the maximum possible out of the other side? I have learned from long experience that the last bit of concession is the most expensive in a negotiation. Invariably, after the negotiation, whether during the final documentation of the deal or after the closing when the buyer finds those unexpected surprises, that the seller who drives the hardest bargain is the one attacked with the most energy by the affronted buyer.

Certainly, sales contracts usually call for a basket or amount of findings below which the buyer will absorb the costs. The problem comes when the buyer finds surprises that could have much greater effect, but whose cost will not be known for years. Customer contracts that come up for renewal but are not renewed as expected, a customer bankruptcy after the closing, a group of employees that leave together to start a new business. There are so many unforeseen opportunities to make a buyer unhappy after the closing, that it is good strategy to leave enough on the table, labeled carefully as such so that there is no doubt as to the "gift" from the seller. As a percentage of the total package, often such a gesture is small, but the benefit can be great if the unexpected happens.

100. Money is not the only measure of success.

You've surely heard of Maslow's Hierarchy of Needs, in which Abraham Maslow laid out a human's needs from the physiological first, to safety, then love and belonging, on to esteem and finally self-actualization. Assuming that you have now passed through the hallowed hall of a successful sale and the money is in the bank, enough to at least temporarily satisfy your needs if not much more. In Maslow's Hierarchy, you have arrived at the point where you can think about love, belonging, esteem and self-actualization.

I have great respect for the young entrepreneur CEO of the game company I described in insight 93, because he disciplined himself enough to take extensive time for family after the closing of the sale, increasing his participation in all things family.

During our business formation years, we pay much more attention to the enterprise than we know we should, at the expense of family and community. I propose that there are few times in life when the opportunity opens to look only outward, to participate in charity events, extended family vacations, community boards and even coaching other entrepreneurs.

If you ever have the opportunity to experience the simple power of having few personal worries, you will have known the freedom of choice that allows you to reinvent yourself, dividing your attention between people and organizations outside of your previous circles. How empowering. And how many organizations are in need of management skills and relationships such as those you could bring, along perhaps with a new focus upon philanthropy.

Maslov demonstrated it as well as can be done. Beyond some point, whatever that is for you, money is not the only measure of success.

101. The most satisfying life journey is never about the money.

As I look back over more than fifty years as an entrepreneur, I can think of the financial focus of my three entrepreneurial businesses as a prime driver in my life during the early stage of each. And yet, as I recall the greatest thrills, the memorable events, the best of memories, almost none are about the money. The stories of people rising to the occasion, victories in the form of great sale successes, great continuing relationships, occasional awards from valued industry or academic institutions, being able to give back to those who appreciate the gift of time or money – all seem to rise well above the feeling recalled about the check or wire transfer that represented a completed sale of a company.

I found one of my joys in angel investing, putting money to work by investing time and money into promising young entrepreneurs much like I once was, coaching them, putting them together with others who have needed skills, helping to build someone else's dream. If you are in such a good place in your life, find a local angel investing group by Googling "angel investing". You will find such a group near enough to drive to their periodic meetings. You'll quickly be drawn into the governance of the organization and introduced into the process of discovery, coaching, leading deals, herding investors, serving on boards and helping entrepreneurs toward liquidity events.

I found another joy in community organizations, joining a total of four non-profit boards, learning at first much more than I could teach, but rising over the years to leadership positions with large psychic rewards along each step of the way.

And then there is family. Be honest with yourself. Have you ever spent enough time with your family? Can you ever? Isn't it time to try?

For those of you still struggling to find that security, to find that balance, I wish you all the skills and all the success possible. For those with the blessing of time and room to breathe, I wish you the wisdom and energy to make use of this most valuable gift. Your most satisfying journey will never be about the money.

About the author...

Dave Berkus has a proven track record in operations, venture investing and corporate board service, both public and private. As an entrepreneur, he has formed, managed and sold successful businesses in the entertainment and software arenas. As a private equity investor, he has obtained healthy returns from liquidity events in over a dozen investments in early-stage ventures. As a corporate mentor and director, he was named *"Director of the Year"* for his directorship efforts with over 40 companies in the past decade.

Dave was the founder of **Computerized Lodging Systems Inc.,** *(CLS),* which he guided as founder and CEO for over a decade that included two consecutive years on the *Inc.500* list of America's fastest growing companies, expansion to six foreign subsidiaries and twenty-nine foreign distributors while capturing 16% of the world market for his enterprise products. Known as a hospitality industry visionary with many "firsts" to his credit, and for his accomplishments in advancing technology in the hospitality industry, in 1998 he was inducted into the **Hospitality (HFTP) "International Hall of Fame"**, one of only twenty-eight so honored worldwide over the years.

He has made over 70 investments in early stage ventures, for which he has an IRR of 97%, which includes capital contributions to his two funds (**Berkus Technology Ventures, LLC** and **Kodiak Ventures, L.P.**, for which he is the managing partner). He is also Chairman Emeritus of the Tech Coast Angels, one of the largest angel networks in the United States.

In recognition for adding significant shareholder value for emerging technology companies over the past decade, he was named **"Director of the Year-Early Stage Businesses"** by the *Forum for Corporate Directors* of Orange County, California. Dave currently sits on ten corporate boards and four non-profit boards.

Dave is also a senior partner in the twenty year old consulting firm of *Hospitality Automation Consultants, LTD (HACL)*, and lends his considerable visionary and strategic talents to worldwide hospitality chains and groups. He is the partner responsible for business process reorganization, strategic planning, software development and wide-area network infrastructure, and enterprise management systems.

A graduate of Occidental College, Dave currently serves as a Trustee of the College. Aside from this book, he is author of *"Extending the Runway"* published by Aspatore Press, and co-author of *"Better Than Money!"* both books for emerging growth technology company executives. Dave serves as Board Member and Vice President of the Western Region*, Boy Scouts of America*, a Board Member of the *Forum for Corporate Directors*, and is Chairman of the Advisory Board of *ABL/TECHNOLOGY*, a networking organization of CEO's in high tech businesses.

He is often engaged as keynote speaker for events worldwide, speaking on trends in technology and of legal and practical issues of governance for emerging company corporate boards.

To contact Mr. Berkus for speaking engagements or workshops, email dberkus@berkus.com , or phone (626)355-5375.

A companion workbook, BERKONOMICS WORKBOOK, is available for purchase from the above website, or the same source as this book.

And a blog, www.Berkonomics.com, contains much of the information from this book with lots of comments from readers with their own stories to tell.

NOTES: